Discussion Pathways to Literacy Learning

Discussion Pathways to Literacy Learning

Thomas M. McCann
Northern Illinois University

Elizabeth A. Kahn
Northern Illinois University

Carolyn C. Walter
Northern Illinois University

NCTE

National Council of Teachers of English
1111 W. Kenyon Road, Urbana, Illinois 61801-1096
www.ncte.org

Staff Editor: Bonny Graham
Manuscript Editor: Josh Rosenberg
Interior Design: Jenny Jensen Greenleaf
Cover Design: Pat Mayer

NCTE Stock Number: 12113; eStock Number: 12120
ISBN 978-0-8141-1211-3; eISBN 978-0-8141-1212-0

Library of Congress Cataloging-in-Publication Data

Names: McCann, Thomas M., author. | Kahn, Elizabeth A., author. | Walter, Carolyn Calhoun, author.
Title: Discussion pathways to literacy learning / Thomas M. McCann, Elizabeth A. Kahn, and Carolyn C. Walter.
Description: Urbana, Illinois : National Council of Teachers of English, [2018] | Includes bibliographical references and index.
Identifiers: LCCN 2018029961 (print) | LCCN 2018050468 (ebook) | ISBN 9780814112120 (ebook) | ISBN 9780814112113 (pbk.) | ISBN 9780814112120 (ebk.)
Subjects: LCSH: Language arts (Secondary) | English language—Study and teaching (Secondary) | College-school cooperation.
Classification: LCC LB1631 (ebook) | LCC LB1631.M275 2018 (print) | DDC 428.4071/2—dc23
LC record available at https://lccn.loc.gov/2018029961

Contents

Acknowledgments

We were able to produce this book only because teachers generously invited us into their classrooms and took time to talk to us about how they do what they do. We are indebted to these admirable colleagues. We are also grateful to the students and their parents for allowing us to record students' classroom discussion and to share with readers some of what they said and wrote. We have protected the identities of the teachers and students whose voices we represent in the book, but we hope nevertheless that they will recognize this acknowledgment as our sincere expression of gratitude.

We also express our gratitude to Northern Illinois University graduate students who served as research assistants for this project. We are especially indebted to Yaqing Cao for transcribing recordings, for assisting in developing and testing a coding system, and for training others to apply the codes to transcribed discussions. We appreciate the efforts of Floyd Knight and Barbara Alvarez in coding transcripts and preparing data for our analysis. We could not have undertaken the research for this book without the assistance of Yaqing, Floyd, and Barbara.

Leaders in the Department of English at Northern Illinois University have supported our research endeavors and have provided the resources necessary for undertaking the recording, transcribing, and analyzing of classroom discussions. We are especially grateful to Lara Crowley, Phil Eubanks, Amy Levin, Bradley Peters, Kathleen Renk, Jessica Reyman, and Mark Van Wienen.

Beyond the high school teachers on whom we focus attention for this book, we acknowledge the benefits of the many opportunities we have had to consult with teachers about the work they do to promote a dialogic classroom. We are especially grateful to Dawn Forde, Joe Flanagan, Andy Bouque, Nicole Boudreau Smith, June Hockison, Barbara Chidley, Greg Lundberg, and Tamara Jaffe Notier.

Students in the Teacher Licensure Program in the Department of English at Northern Illinois University developed some of the problem-based cases discussed in this book. We appreciate the efforts of our students as they sought to discover what problems resonate with adolescents and what forums invited engaged participation in discussion.

We are grateful to Michael W. Smith for his foreword. As usual, Michael's writing is insightful, touching, and generous. We also appreciate the ongoing conversations we have had with friends and colleagues about the themes and research protocols for this book. We always benefit from our conversation with our old friend Peter Smagorinsky and with our university colleagues John V. Knapp, Judy Pokorny, Laura Bird, Jeff Levin, and Marilee Halpin. We appreciate also the support of Pam McCann and Katie Carlson as they listened patiently to descriptions of plans and our reactions to discoveries.

We appreciate the dedicated work of Kurt Austin and Bonny Graham at NCTE, and the other contributors to the production process, including copy editor Joshua Rosenberg.

Foreword

Michael W. Smith
Temple University

A story to start. When my niece Kelsy, my mom's oldest grandchild, was three or so, she went to Sunday school for the first time. As one might expect, she was very excited to be going, and indeed that excitement was evident when she invited my mom on the afternoon of her very first day of class to come over to play school. Of course, my mom could hardly say no, so off she went. Kelsy had everything waiting for her in the living room, having set up a chair right in front of Kelsy's chalkboard.

"Have a seat, everyone," Kelsy said, so my mom sat down. Kelsy got down to business right away: "Now, Grandma, can you tell me the first book of the Bible?"

My mom, no biblical scholar, replied, "Exodus."

"WRONG!" Kelsy shouted. "It's Genesis."

This little story has been the stuff of legends in my family for what it says about Kelsy's precocity. But when I look back on it now, I think it's more telling for what it says about school. You see, Kelsy had been to school for little more than an hour and she already knew that what teachers do is ask their students fact-based questions that students often get wrong so teachers have to correct them.

Kelsy's playacting with my mom demonstrates why the project McCann, Kahn, and Walter take up in this book is so very important. A wealth of research clearly establishes that classrooms in general and English classrooms in particular are much more apt to be characterized by Kelsy-like recitations than they are by the kind of generative conversations that the authors share with us throughout the book. A wealth of research also establishes that those kinds of generative conversations have far-reaching benefits for students.

But knowing the problem doesn't mean it's easily solved. Another story. Not long after I got my PhD, I had the privilege of serving as a research assistant on Arthur Applebee's (1989) study of the teaching of literature in programs with reputations for excellence. One of my tasks was to take a log of class activities in the classes I observed. Though I did the work thirty years ago, I will never forget one of my observations, a whole-class discussion of *A Tale of Two Cities*. The teacher clearly loved the book and was trying to communicate that love to his students. He fired off question after question and students offered brief replies. Sometimes in his enthusiasm he interrupted his students before they finished those brief replies so he could make a point. I estimated that he spoke about 95 percent of the words during the class. After class was over, I asked one of the questions on the interview protocol, something like this: "How does what I saw today compare to your typical class?" His response: "We have this kind of scintillating conversation nearly every day."

That teacher could not have been more dedicated. He could not have known and cared about his content any more deeply. But he also couldn't have mischaracterized his class any more completely. And he's not alone. Indeed, even teachers who are committed to classroom discourse that resembles a "jam session" (Marshall, Smagorinsky, & Smith, 1995, p. 19) are undone by their concern that their discussions "get somewhere," typically to some kind of shared interpretative understanding.

Moreover, Kamil and his colleagues (2008) speculate that teachers may not have the skills they need to guide productive discussion. I've been teaching for more than forty years now, and I regularly have the experience of asking a question that is met with empty stares or of receiving an unexpected response and not knowing what to say.

So what to do? My answer in short is to read this book, for it does a better job than any book of which I am aware of providing an alternative to the patterns of discourse that typify discussions in the English language arts. The book achieves this crucially important goal in a radical way: by recasting teachers not as question-askers but rather as problem-posers.

McCann, Kahn, and Walter demonstrate what can happen when teachers engage students in thinking hard about complex problems that have multiple sustainable positions as a way to foster critical thinking, talking, and writing that will prepare students for extended inquiries. They demonstrate how these inquiries can, in turn, provide a context in which crucially important knowledge, skills, and strategies can be both developed and rewarded.

Recasting the teacher's role as a problem-poser rather than as a question-asker challenges the norms of classroom discussion. Since Mehan's (1979) foundational research, the field has known that discussions in school are patterned: The teacher initiates an exchange with a question, a student responds to that question, and then the floor returns to the teacher who provides an evaluation or, as Marshall, Smagorinsky, and Smith (1995) found, an elaboration. When teachers build their discussion around questions, that pattern is cued. I think of the issue in terms of Maslow's (1966) famous rumination: "I suppose it is tempting, if the only tool you have is a hammer, to treat everything as if it were a nail" (p. 15). The analog to Maslow's comment might read, "If the only tool that you have is a question, everything starts to look like an answer." That is, questions cue recitations while problems don't. Just take a quick look at any of the excerpts that McCann, Kahn, and Walter provide. What you see is students taking extended turns in which they articulate and support their claims. Just take a quick look at Figure 5.8. What you see is a picture that clearly shows that when students are given generative problems they talk to one another and not just to their teachers.

McCann, Kahn, and Walter provide multiple examples that demonstrate that this picture can be realized across grades, tracks, and school and subject contexts. But they do much more than simply illustrate what classroom discussions can look like. They go to great lengths to articulate the meticulous planning that accounted for those illustrations. They share how they identified problems that are compelling to students. They talk about how to build those problems into complex cases. They explain moves teachers can make within discussions to foster authentic conversations. They share a planning heuristic and scales that teachers can use to assess their own and their students' performance. They demonstrate how one can use the problems to introduce larger units of study. Their work gives their readers not only ready-to-use tools but also understandings that can be adapted for whatever teaching context we find ourselves in.

McCann, Kahn, and Walter also give us another great gift. As they point out, in this era of high-stakes testing and teacher accountability, too often we lose sight of what brought us to the profession in the first place: the joy of thinking and talking and reading and writing with others about issues that matter. When I read the transcripts and the essays that McCann, Kahn, and Walter share, I saw that joy manifested. Any teacher or prospective teacher who reads this book will be far more likely both to experience that joy themselves and to be able to share that joy with their students.

References

Applebee, A. (1989). *The teaching of literature in programs with reputations for excellence in English* (Technical Report No. 1.1). Albany: University at Albany, State University of New York, Center for the Learning and Teaching of Literature.

Kamil, M. L., Borman, G. D., Dole, J., Kral, C. C., Salinger, T., & Torgesen, J. (2008). *Improving adolescent literacy: Effective classroom and intervention practices: A practice guide* (NCEE #2008-4027). Washington, DC: National Center for Education Evaluation and Regional Assistance, Institute of Education Sciences, US Department of Education. Retrieved from http://ies.ed.gov/ncee/wwc (https://ies.ed.gov/ncee/wwc/Docs/PracticeGuide/adlit_pg_082608.pdf).

Marshall, J. D., Smagorinsky, P., & Smith, M. W. (1995). *The language of interpretation: Patterns of discourse in discussions of literature.* Urbana, IL: National Council of Teachers of English.

Maslow, A. H. (1966). *The psychology of science: A reconnaissance.* New York: Harper & Row.

Mehan, H. (1979). *Learning lessons: Social organization in the classroom.* Cambridge, MA: Harvard University Press.

1

Let's Talk about Talk in the Classroom

After observing some high school classes engaged in intense and sustained discussions about complex issues, we have sought to understand how a teacher can consistently engage students enthusiastically in talking about substantive topics, including the interpretation of texts. We have observed classes in which the students facilitated the discussions and did almost all of the talking. As we share below, we have also observed classes in which students tackled contentious issues, even issues that many teachers would shy away from introducing to their classes. We knew that if we were going to prepare new teachers to enter classrooms ready to rely on substantive talk to foster literacy learning and critical thinking, we would need to know what practices distinguish teachers who engage students in consequential conversations and shared inquiry.

We begin with Ms. Widerhaken's class of eleventh graders in an urban high school, where the students had been discussing the challenges that teachers in a neighboring state had faced when they introduced their students to the concept of *white privilege* as part of a "diversity unit" in social studies classes. The students in Ms. Widerhaken's class read about the case and about similar situations in other schools. They entered into a discussion about the necessity and appropriateness of teaching the concept in their own school. Here is a small part of the exchange:

SILVIA: I don't feel like you cannot build a relationship across races. For everyone who looks at white people, that they are bad also, I don't feel like every white person is horrible, just like I don't think every black person is poor. I still feel like that it should be taught. You are going to think how you want about these things. Some people look at white people like they are all bad. I feel bad right now in this class saying that "white people, white people, white people." You don't know how you would feel towards whites.

RAYMOND: I think it [bigotry] can change but not immediately change. I think it takes more time than what we usually have left. We are still young but I don't think it can change by that time. I don't know like you said everybody should believe in changing. I still don't think it will change right now. Our kids' kids can see the change but not us.

MS. WIDERHAKEN: What else?

STUART: He said that our kids' kids will see the change. But I don't think the world is that bad.

DARNELL: I believe that we can at least start the change because teaching the next generation about it makes them do more than we could have done in our lifetime and make them keep going on and make this world a better place.

RAYMOND: This white privilege thing, has been going for how long? I don't know. It has been a long time, though. I think it is even going to take even longer for the world to come together.

SHANICE: I say I don't really want to do this [study the concept of white privilege] because at the bottom, people are already constricting. They've already found their opinions that blacks are already having a weak heart. So that I don't think people are going to change what they believe. On bottom, I am going to tell my parents like, "You have to go and talk what you want because people love to believe what they want. They can be secure and they can be higher, though, as a white person. People are already knowing what they believe."

JASMINE: I feel like we are the first who are going to try to change this. We've already had people who feel so positive that black and white people work together. Now we are all together. So we work together and go to school together. What I have trouble understanding is what has changed them because like I just don't understand that because we've already communicated with each other, having black and white progressing together. I don't get it. OK, you can see for many times that they are all equal or like you can make posters. I don't understand how it is going. I just don't get it. I just don't understand why you feel like completely pained. People are already believing what they believe. It seems very impossible because, think about it, we had Martin Luther King and others. We have you. We have everybody. I mean, I don't understand. I need the right people. I don't understand.

SILVIA: I feel like it is kind of our fault. I don't feel like it is white people's fault. It is our fault because some kids are different. I can go to the same store and she goes too and be treated the same way. You see, it is our problem. Around here, you don't see a lot of white people being mean. But some people do that because they have been brought up that way. They are still bad.

SHANICE: It is also about where you come from. A lot of times, it is not just black people and that white aren't that saggy, most of the time. If you are saggy, then it is bound that they come from the hood. White people who do come from the hood, they are saggy just like us. But you have white people come of advantage to that race, the top white. The white people that come from the hood, they are saggy just like us.

The discussions about the prospect of teaching high school students about white privilege spanned three class meetings, following a carefully devised sequence. As we witnessed the discussions and revisited them through analysis of the transcripts, we noted how deeply involved students were in the discussions. We were also struck by how students, as they talked, engaged in several important intellectual and literacy moves, usually associated with "college readiness": supporting claims with evidence, citing texts and explaining the citations, representing and building on the comments of others, evaluating claims, connecting arguments, summarizing, and arguing for a specific policy. Ms. Widerhaken's class, and similar high school classes we have observed as part of our research into classroom discourse, exhibited evidence of the two daily goals we have had in our combined 120+ years of teaching English: that students learn something and have a positive experience doing it, even when discussions become heated and topics are emotionally charged and hard to talk about.

In this book, we profile some teachers who have developed particular skills at engaging students in inquiry and sustained discussion in support of that inquiry and as part of the processes of learning to write elaborated compositions and read complex texts. We have observed the teachers and their students in classrooms in schools that were quite distinct from each other. Our observations have been part of a long effort to understand how teachers can engage students in sustained discussions that the learners find exhilarating as they learn some sophisticated procedures for critical thought and for advanced literacy practices.

The State of Classroom Discussion

In the 1990s, Martin Nystrand and a team of researchers at the University of Wisconsin observed teachers and students in scores of classrooms across three states. In his report, Nystrand (1997) distinguishes *authentic discussion* as discussion about questions that do not have prespecified answers. To illustrate, imagine the following exchange in a World History class that had been studying the French Revolution and Louis the XVI's attempt to escape with his life.

TEACHER: When King Louis escaped, where did he go?

STUDENT: England.

TEACHER: No.

STUDENT: Germany.

TEACHER: No. Think about Marie Antoinette.

STUDENT: Austria.

TEACHER: Austria. Right. And will this make things better or worse for Louis?

STUDENT: Worse.

TEACHER: Worse. That's right.

Perhaps the interchange in this format was necessary to assess what students could recall about the events in history, but you could hardly call it an open exchange of ideas in a process of constructing deep understanding about the political, cultural, and economic factors that fomented revolution and fostered a reign of terror. In many ways, the teacher signals to the students that they are expected to recite what the teacher already knows: He opens with a question that has a clear answer. He coaxes students to narrow their choices. He offers the last question as a selection between two possibilities. While such brief exchanges might serve a purpose, they are hardly engaging for learners and offer little to help them construct their own understandings: They are simply reciting from recall, or guessing from the clues the teacher offers.

If practices have not changed much since Nystrand's 1997 study—and, in fact, Nystrand (2017) reports that over three decades classroom discussion "has only declined as an instructional activity"—then the recitation episode above is typical of what an observer would find in a history or English class in middle school or high school today. Nystrand (1997) reports that in the scores of schools he studied, authentic discussion occupied, on average, a mere fifteen seconds per class meeting in ninth grade. We will refer to this startling statistic again and again in this book as a point of contrast. We find it a troubling statistic because it means that students, who typically take delight in interacting with their peers, have a mostly passive role in the classroom where the teacher does most of the talking.

The Impact of Authentic Discussion

We report ruefully that the students in the Nystrand study seldom participated in authentic discussion. But why should we care? If discussion is not a dominant feature of instruction in middle school and high school classrooms, can't students learn much in a variety of other ways? We know that students learn through a variety of experiences and activity structures. We have seen evidence that students have learned much through dramatic presentations, artistic representations of complex concepts, self-directed learning modules, and individual research. But we also know that engagement in authentic discussion leads to high levels of learning, especially literacy learning. Nystrand (1997) found a strong positive correlation between participation in discussion and performance on measures of achievement in reading and writing.

Researchers at the University of Michigan's School of Education identify discussion as a "high leverage practice," one leading to substantial student learning and essential for advancing skills in teaching: "The purposes of a discussion are to build collective knowledge and capability in relation to specific instructional goals and to allow students to practice listening, speaking, and interpreting" (n.p.). Nystrand (2006) reports that extensive participation in authentic discussion has a positive impact on reading comprehension. Applebee, Langer, Nystrand, and Gamoran (2003) report that in classrooms where teachers followed discussion-based approaches, students performed better on measures of achievement than did peers who did not experience such instruction. Langer (2001) reports that in schools that "beat the odds," students frequently participated in both small group and whole class discussions. Hattie's (2009) synthesis of more than 800 meta-analyses reports shifts in student learning and achievement in terms of *effect size*, a summary measure of growth, with standard deviation being the unit of measure. Simply put, a positive shift in performance from pre-test to post-test of nearly +1.00 would be evidence of significant growth. In looking at general trends across studies, Hattie reports that the effect size for classroom discussion was 0.82, well beyond his reported "hinge point" of 0.40, the average across more than 140,000 effect sizes, making classroom discussion indeed a "high leverage practice."

The large effect size from classroom discussion makes good sense when we see learning as socially situated. Vygotsky (1996) reminds us that learning is a social experience: "Unlike the development of instincts, thinking and behavior of adolescents are prompted not from within but from without, by the social milieu" (108). The interactions with others have a powerful impact, in everything from defining relatively simple concepts (e.g., distinguishing one fruit from another) to assessing the advantages and disadvantages associated with several possible courses of action in order to recommend and defend a specific policy. Bakhtin (1986) observes that much thought—"philosophical, scientific, artistic—is born of the process of interaction and struggle with others' thought" (p. 92). We judge that when students in middle school and high school grapple with each other in trying to understand complex concepts, including interpretations of literature and decisions about thorny policy questions, they learn more than the recall of information, although recall is likely to serve analyses. We have witnessed repeatedly instances when students have noted that they have entered class firm in their positions about issues and shifted their positions as classmates challenged them, offered alternatives, tested assumptions by citing exceptions to rules, and expressed reasonable arguments. We see such flexibility as a necessary habit of mind for entering the intellectual conversations of the university; making decisions at home, on the job, and in the community; and simply thinking about the issues of the day.

Kuhn (1991) and Mercier and Sperber (2011, 2017) report that most often humans draw conclusions first and then search for the support for the positions that they are predisposed to embrace, leading some people to watch only Fox News and ignore MSNBC, or vice versa. But, if teachers want students to assume an academic intellectual position, they will want the learners to recognize and evaluate a variety of opinions to arrive at a deeper understanding of a complex issue, or at least to espouse positions supported by reason rather than advanced as a prejudice.

Sherry Turkle (2015) worries about the decline in conversation as a result of the distractions from and dependence on technology. She sees value in face-to-face talk that goes beyond ramping up scores on achievement tests: "Many of the things we all struggle with in love and work can be helped by conversation. Without conversation, studies show that we are less empathic, less connected, less creative and fulfilled" (p. 13). She cites philosopher Heinrich von Kleist to point to conversation's benefits as a means for exploring ideas and refining understandings. Turkle observes, "The best thoughts, in his view, can be almost unintelligible as they emerge; what matters most is risky, thrilling conversation as a crucible for discovery" (p. 37). Our work over many years has been an attempt to use classroom conversation as a vehicle for learning and as a mode of school experience that can be exhilarating and satisfying for all involved.

Joy: The Unstated Goal

Over our careers, we have observed in hundreds of classrooms. As supervisors in high schools, as supervisors of student teachers, and as consultants working in several states, we have been in many classrooms, across several subject areas. In the classrooms we have visited, rarely do teachers say explicitly what the learning target is for a specific lesson. Most often we have observed teachers launch into an activity without connecting it to previous class meetings and without explicitly identifying its purpose. In some cases, however, a teacher will write objectives on the board, including the related Common Core State Standard. In fact, in some schools, teachers are required to write the learning objectives on the board in the form of "I can" statements, as students' affirmations, as in "I can cite evidence from a text to support a claim," or "I can identify the climax in a short story." Never have we seen anyone, including ourselves, write something like this on the board: "Everyone will enjoy the experiences in this class today."

Even though we don't see such statements posted for students to see, we hope and believe that most teachers enter the classroom with the expectation that students will take some joy in their learning. To a certain extent, this pleasure goal still drives what we do with students today, and we know that the exhilaration that learners might experience is reciprocal: If they are enjoying their learning experience, we will take joy in their pleasure. We have seen such intentions pursued in various ways among other teachers.

We know two teachers who have worked for years as partners in teaching an interdisciplinary class in a high school. We will call the course Western World Studies. The teachers pride themselves on their creativity, and they work hard to find ways to engage adolescent learners. But our best intentions sometimes go awry; and when they do, we can reflect on what went wrong to judge how to refine practice. We can think of two well-intentioned examples.

In an effort to engage students in learning about cultures of the Middle East during the Middle Ages, the teachers (whom we will call Mr. Gordon and Ms. Amari) staged a simulated "Middle Eastern bazaar" where merchants met at a crossroads to display and peddle their wares. Each team of students was assigned a role—e.g., spice merchant, rug merchant, clothier, jeweler, potter—and directed to research the role of this merchant in society and the goods that the merchant would likely have for sale. The teachers had reserved the high school's multipurpose room and constructed makeshift tents to serve as the vendors' booths. The teachers encouraged students to dress as they imagined Middle Eastern merchants of the Middle Ages might dress. On the day of the bazaar, the students in their roles as merchants assumed a position in front of a tent where they would rely on a small stack of index cards to explain to the passing "customers" (played by classmates) who they were and describe the goods they had to offer. Classmates took turns in rotating through the bazaar to hear all of the presentations and take notes. The activity, with its simulation, movement, costumes, and trappings of place, would seem to be highly engaging for students; but the learners essentially moved around a room and listened to brief lectures by inexperienced lecturers, with the goal in the end to recall bits of information.

In a second effort, Ms. Amari and Mr. Gordon hoped for their students to learn something about the structure of medieval European society. Toward this end, they invited the members of the school's chess team to teach the students the basic moves of chess. One class meeting was taken up with a presentation and demonstration of the basic moves and strategies of chess. When the class met again, the teachers distributed several chess sets, paired students, and set them to playing chess for approximately twenty minutes. After the students had experienced a chess game for a time, the teachers directed the students to take out their journals and respond in writing to this question: How does the game of chess symbolically represent the hierarchy of medieval European society? The students looked stunned and then scanned the room to see if anyone else knew how to respond. After a few students complained that they did not know what to write, the teachers told the class that it was time to stop complaining and to start writing. Since few students seemed to be writing anything, Ms. Amari and Mr. Gordon soon interrupted to ask students to share their interpretations of the symbols. A couple of students made bold attempts, but most reported that they had no idea of the connection between the chess pieces and the narrative they had been asked to read in their history text. The teachers gently scolded the students for not being able to make the connections and were left with dictating to the students the conclusions that they should have reached.

The teachers cared for their students and cared for the quality of their experience in the classroom. The activities that they had planned seemed to have promise: There was a game and play, students interacted with a partner, and the learners had an opportunity to discover and construct meaning. There were at least two obvious problems: (1) The students were not prepared sufficiently to be able to make the leap into symbolic thinking, either because they really knew very little about medieval European society, or they made no connection between the highly abstract game and the details of the historical world. (2) The teachers had made no genuine "dialogic bid," as Nystrand (1997) calls it, to signal to the students that the symbolic conclusions were open to interpretation: It was clear from the journal prompt that the teachers already had a specific interpretation in mind.

As Ms. Amari and Mr. Gordon demonstrate, it is easy to fool ourselves that the discourse in our classrooms is largely dialogic, and it is easy to misjudge what problems will resonate with students and what activities will provide a quality experience. We know that Ms. Amari and Mr. Gordon are reflective enough to see that the outcomes for their lessons were not what they had planned, and they amended their plans to be both more engaging and more dialogic. The business of authentic discussion, while seemingly intuitive and simple, is rather complicated, as we demonstrate throughout this book, and the process of providing learners with exhilarating and memorable classroom experiences is not an exact science. But for students to engage in inquiry and discussions, the problems at the heart of the inquiry must resonate with the learners and seem of some consequence. To a certain extent, students as a body should have some choice in the line of inquiry they pursue as a community (cf. Stern, 1995). That is just a start. Students must see that they each have as much knowledge and voice as any of their peers to contribute to a group effort to think about the problem and its potential solutions. Each student should feel valued in the classroom and able to take some intellectual risks without fearing ridicule and suppression. The structures for inquiry and discussion should build upon themselves so the discussions of today prepare for the discussions tomorrow, which in turn prepare for subsequent reading, writing, and further discussions. The frequent interactions as a common element of daily experience in the classroom should ultimately build a sense of community, a connectedness among peers within the classroom and across the school. These elements—problem-solving with everyday or "real world" problems, a voice in choosing what to study, a sense of efficacy, and a feeling of community—are basic to human motivation and help to foster satisfaction with the experience of school.

We think that allowing students to engage with one another about issues that matter to the learners is a key element in bringing some joy into the experience of learning in the English language arts classroom. Various thinkers have said more or less the same thing. Linda Christensen (2009) seeks to celebrate students' lives, language, and stories through a process of seeking justice: "Teaching for joy and justice means creating a curriculum that matters, a curriculum that helps students make sense of the world, that makes them feel smart—educated even" (p. 7). Wilhelm, Fransen, and Smith (2014) support students' experiencing the joy of reading by entering into the texts that most appeal to their interests and by sharing with friends the multiple pleasures of reading. Wilhelm and Novak (2011) seek to help students read and respond to literature in ways that are transformative and that lead ultimately to connecting with a community and feeling a part of an associated life. Similarly, Wilhelm and his colleagues Whitney Douglas and Sara W. Fry (2014) offer many ways in which students can find joy through service to others. Garcia and O'Donnell-Allen (2015) suggest a variety of ways in which teachers can assume new stances ("poses") to upset the conventional teaching and learning experiences, ultimately to bring joy to students. In all these cases, teachers strive to make learning purposeful and meaningful for adolescents. Students engage with ideas that matter, and their purposeful inquiries with peers support them to persist with tough reading and to endeavor to share in writing their stand on issues that matter.

The Discussion of Discussion in This Book

Throughout this book, we examine the practices of several high school English teachers who have been kind enough to allow us to observe in their classrooms and to talk to them at length about what they do to invite students to talk to each other in the classroom for the purposes of literacy learning and critical thinking. As our review above reveals, it is critically important that a teacher of English knows how to facilitate discussion as an essential tool for literacy instruction. Research, as well as our own experience and observations over many years, reveals that consistently facilitating authentic discussion in most classrooms is not easy and not "natural" for most teachers; it requires procedural knowledge, practice, reflection, and problem-solving. We agree with Britton (1983) that "reading and writing float on a sea of talk" (p. 11). But we want teachers to have a keen sense of what students do when they engage with each other in purposeful conversation, both in the classroom and in a digital environment. We also want teachers to be well aware of what especially reflective teachers do when they plan discussion-based instruction and when they facilitate discussion from day to day.

We begin with a teacher who prepares students to assume the responsibility for discussion, with astounding results. The next chapter accounts for a process of preparing students for discussion, shows students at work, and reports the outcomes of their extensive talk. As we report in detail later, for two class meetings the students did almost all of the talking, focused entirely on the topic at hand, and were supportive and inclusive toward all speakers. Our observations in this one classroom prompted this big question: What factors account for the wide and lively participation of students and their extensive contributions? Were these particularly gifted students in an exclusive school? Was the topic itself the key to prompting discussion? Did the structure of the sequence of discussion activities foster earnest participation? Was this an unusually skilled teacher?

The Power of Classroom Conversations

Learning

Extensive classroom discussions

- **Engage** learners in key procedures that transfer to writing
- **Serve** as preparation for elaborated writing
- **Motivate** students to read, research, and write
- **Foster** interpretations and critical assessments of complex texts

Feeling

Extensive classroom discussions

- **Encourage** students to share with peers
- **Affirm** students' knowledge and voice
- **Foster** discovery of new possibilities
- **Inspire** learners to take action to ameliorate problems

Acting

Extensive classroom discussions

- **Encourage** students to collaborate in problem-solving and discovery
- **Invite** multiple participants in conversations
- **Affirm** value in differences
- **Build** a collaborative community

To a certain extent, we can say "all of the above" to account for the factors that fostered authentic discussion. But the process of planning and facilitation cannot remain a mystery if other teachers are going to be able to replicate what we saw in a classroom where students were learning much and enjoying their experience. In Chapter 3, we compare classrooms across settings: small town, suburban, and urban. Our intention is to check on several factors: Does discussion depend on being in the right school in the right setting with the right kids? Are only teachers with special gifts and talents able to foster authentic discussion? Is hitting on the hot button topic the key to it all? Can a teacher design discussion activities in such a way that there is a reasonable guarantee of wide and engaged participation?

In part, the evidence we have seen of students' willing participation in a connected series of discussions is the result of the teachers' careful planning. Perhaps there are teachers who can enter classrooms each day equipped with little more than a provocative question and set off an intense discussion. In contrast, the teachers we have observed have planned carefully to be sure that students are prepared to discuss across a connected sequence, both for working on a problem during the current week of lessons and for applying the same intellectual moves and protocols in future discussions. In Chapter 4 we follow the planning processes and reveal teachers' thinking about fostering a sense of support and civility.

Chapter 5 reveals teachers' practices in the classroom. These practices include the yearlong attention to the tone in the classroom, the sense of community, and the established protocols for engaging with each other, even when problems are emotionally charged. We also look at teachers' moves from moment to moment in the classroom to unveil the seeming mystery behind those teachers who are able to get kids talking when others can't. Authentic discussion is by its nature an ill-structured problem. Although it is not possible to map out a flowchart or define a formula to reveal the decisions a teacher should make to initiate, extend, evaluate, and connect discussions, we do generalize about the practices that are likely to invite students into consequential instructional conversations.

Throughout the book, we report our classroom observations when teachers were engaging learners in discussions that led to writing and served as a gateway into a larger line of inquiry. In Chapter 6, we discuss the follow-through for these discussions. The gateway activity would have limited impact if the students were not able to connect these early discussions to their subsequent discussions about literature, film, and other texts. We value coherence and shared inquiry, which require planning, adjustments, and attention to the connections across texts and their related discussion.

We conclude with our observations about the impact that discussion appears to have had on the learners we have observed, including apparent literacy learning and a general satisfaction about being a participant in an English class. We generalize also about the practices that should serve teachers in most settings in initiating, managing, assessing, sustaining, and connecting authentic discussions as key elements in the process of inquiry and literacy learning.

2

Finding Pleasures in Literacy Learning

Referring to their 2002 research into literacy in the lives of adolescent males, Michael W. Smith and Jeffrey Wilhelm (2010) recall an interview with a student they call Buda, who notes his resistance to the tasks his English teacher sets for him: "I'm not going to do this crap. . . . The teacher wouldn't do this crap!" (p. 9). We couldn't help but think of this reaction when we reviewed some of the lesson plans that a group of preservice teachers had devised. New to their teacher preparation program and with limited experience in facilitating lessons with any middle school or high school students, the preservice teachers understandably seemed a bit naïve about the likely reception from the classes of adolescents. Some of the lessons struck us as quite distinct from, and much less engaging than, the models the preservice teachers saw in their readings or that we had modeled in class. We worried that these inexperienced teachers would be in a vulnerable state if they encountered a resistant group of adolescents who saw the prescribed literacy tasks as dull and inconsequential, to use more delicate descriptors than Buda used. We wanted to awaken the novices to the idea that the quality of experience for everyone and the likelihood of any significant literacy learning would result only if the learners saw the instructional activities as meaningful and somewhat enjoyable—that the activities helped them to learn something they valued and they had some fun in the process.

Authentic and Enjoyable as a Standard

When we visit middle school and high school classrooms, we sometimes see the learning "targets" for the current lesson written on the board, sometimes in the required form of "I can" statements and sometimes in the language of the Common Core State Standards (CCSS). Though, as explained in Chapter 1, we have yet to see the goal that students enjoy their experience in class directly stated as an objective or "learning target" for the day, we intended to sensitize the emerging teachers in our program to the idea that the learning can and should be enjoyable, partly because students have chances to engage with their peers and partly because the problems at the heart of instructional activities seem of some consequence to the learners. To begin, we surveyed two classes of preservice English teachers, asking them to rate each item in a list of common learning activities in two ways: (1) To what extent does this represent the kind of activity in which you engage as a mature and literate thinker? (2) To what extent would you enjoy this kind of experience? They responded to each of the choices on a four-point scale: Frequently, Occasionally, Seldom, or Never.

For the activity descriptors, we drew from the lessons that the preservice teachers had written and from the examples in the texts that they were studying. The list ranged from vocabulary worksheets to note-taking, and from PowerPoint presentations to dramatic performances of scenes from literature. While the list was far from exhaustive, it offered contrasts in choices for activity structures and allowed the preservice teachers to reflect on which activities they would actually do themselves and might even enjoy. In addition to offering a list of choices, we invited students to add any other enjoyable possibilities that they could think of. We received only one additional suggestion: "discussion with friends."

We hoped that their responses and reflections would lead these preservice teachers to some self-consciousness about assigning adolescents tasks that they themselves would not enjoy and would probably not realistically participate in as highly literate adults. In other words, we wanted our students to judge the extent to which common learning activities could be both *authentic* and *enjoyable*. The clear preferences were those activities that introduced a problem (e.g., scenario, case study, dramatic performance) and allowed peers to talk with each other about their responses to the problem. The problem could be a "real world" situation that one might see in a news story, or a fictional representation of a problem seen in several news stories. The problem could also involve a question of interpretation or appreciation—like watching a film or listening to music and talking about it with friends. The clearly less preferable activities were those that seemed like teacher-imposed tasks, usually done independently and with no clear connection to other elements of the class. These included "vocabulary squares," other vocabulary study (presumably out of context), worksheets, and word searches. In sharing these results with the preservice teachers, we asked them to consider this question: As you design instructional activities for adolescent learners, why would you impose an activity that you would not enjoy yourself and would not likely do as a highly literate person?

The survey results revealed which *categories* or *types* of activities learners would likely see as meaningful and potentially enjoyable. The problem remained to design specific activities aligned with specific learning goals and meeting the needs of a specific group of learners. In a class in the Teaching of

Writing, students typically produced a prewriting or *gateway* activity (Hillocks, 1995), usually one that prepares students to write argument, especially a composition that also connects with the literature that a middle school or high school class is exploring. Our idea has been to work collaboratively as a methods class to construct one gateway activity to model for preservice teachers the process of designing such learning experiences. Each preservice teacher or teams of preservice teachers then follow the same procedures and construct new gateway activities to teach in a clinical setting.

Asking What Resonates

In designing a gateway activity that fits into one of the high-ranking categories from our informal survey of our methods students, we still had to find a problem that seemed to resonate with adolescents. While we could make reasonable conjectures—many of the preservice teachers, after all, were not far from adolescence—we thought it wise to run some possibilities by actual teens, recognizing that learners benefit from inquiry into problems that they find meaningful (Stern, 1995). Culling recent news stories, we saw several problems that might potentially resonate with teens. These would be debatable cases that could be argued from multiple points of view, with sufficient connections to the lives of teens and the literature that they were reading in school. Six of the situations we discovered became the basis for another survey, one that ninth and tenth graders in two different high schools (one urban, one suburban) completed, with the cooperation and support of their teachers. We asked the high school students to complete a ballot by judging each problem summary on a four-point scale:

> 4 = This story interests me, and I am eager to talk about it with my friends and classmates.
>
> 3 = This story holds some interest, and I wouldn't mind talking about it with my classmates.
>
> 2 = This story is only marginally interesting, and I could be encouraged to talk about it with classmates.
>
> 1 = This story doesn't interest me at all, and I would find it annoying to talk about it.

Here is a brief summary of the six debatable problems presented in the survey:

> *The Krampus:* In Bavaria, the Krampus is a legendary figure that represents a counterpart to Santa Claus. A shaggy, horned, and fanged creature, the Krampus frightens children into behaving so they will be worthy of presents at Christmas. Residents of a town in south central Pennsylvania want to take up the Krampus tradition, possibly with some nightmarish consequences.
>
> *Sell Art to Save a School:* A financially faltering parochial school is considering selling some of the valuable art in its collection to prop up the school's budget. Some alumni and parents see this as a foolhardy stopgap measure.
>
> *Suppress the Fighting:* Critics want to rewrite the school's fight song so it emphasizes struggle and cooperation and does not encourage violence. This change will be a challenge to a long tradition and perhaps undermine freedom of expression.
>
> *Save the Doctor:* A medical doctor has emerged physically depleted from a US hospital after he was treated for Ebola. Against the objections of loved ones, the doctor wants to return to West Africa to continue to serve Ebola patients.
>
> *Directing an Old Film:* Scores of preserved reels of legendary director Orson Welles's last film have been secured by film enthusiasts who plan to do the final editing to produce a completed film. Those who oppose this project challenge the presumption of others to assume the role of the great director.
>
> *The Robot Teacher:* A school board can land a grant to purchase two robot teachers for a pilot study in their school. Critics resist the idea that a robot can assume this uniquely human role.

The students in the ninth-and tenth-grade classes surveyed overwhelmingly preferred to talk about the prospect of a robot teacher. Indeed, there was a significant difference among the story choices, across the respondents in each of three classes. The response to the robot teacher problem was significantly different from the responses to all of the other stories, except the story about the doctor recovering from Ebola. Interestingly, the two top-ranking stories have to do with relationships: the teacher to the students and their families; the doctor to loved ones and the patients he might continue to serve. The survey results suggest that either story has potential for stimulating extensive discussion that would lead to elaborated writing. We chose the apparent favorite and organized the preservice teachers to write the full case as a series of detailed lesson plans that the partner high school teachers could follow with their students.

Planning Instructional Experiences

Following the role-playing models suggested by Troyka and Nudelman (1975) and McCann (2014), we offered the preservice teachers a template that prompted them to contribute to the design of the lesson: a narrative of the problem; attention to potentially unfamiliar vocabulary; descriptions of six characters invested in the outcome of the case; a data set to support problem-solving; identification of related articles that students might consult; directions for small group discussion, role-playing deliberation, and whole class debriefing; a prompt and accompanying rubric for a written response; and a list of related texts to explore as extensions of the current inquiry.

The class at the university divided into six teams, with each team tackling a different part of the overall task. We reproduce here the basic elements of the case they designed. We have left out some of the details (e.g., academic vocabulary, detailed character descriptions, rubric for the written product) that serve a purpose for the teachers in training who are required to compile portfolios with artifacts that reveal their attention to various standards.

Brave New Classroom

Background: There already are robot bartenders and driverless cars, so it should come as no surprise that the Huxley Corporation has produced a *robot teacher.* The designers call the current model *Alpha Master 84.* While quite advanced compared to earlier attempts, the Alpha Master models are still in a developmental stage and are quite expensive. Although the Huxley designers acknowledge that the Alpha Master 84 requires further refinement, they insist that it is far more advanced than the primitive prototypes that other companies have placed in a few school settings to date. The Foundation for Liberty and Prosperity has agreed to fund the piloting of the use of five robot teachers at Floodrock High School, if the school board requests this grant. If the seven members of the school board agree, in the coming school year, the five Alpha Masters will teach US history, beginning Chinese, and three different math classes. The manufacturer claims that the robot teachers never tire, lose patience, get distracted, nor disseminate inaccuracies. They monitor and record students' behavior constantly, attend unremittingly to provisions for students' special needs, and communicate with parents quickly and frequently. Each Alpha Master will be able to communicate with students at any time of the day or night and will have a vast storehouse of resources, models, and materials to share instantly with each student.

Some skepticism: Some traditionalists and the local teachers' union resist this move and fear that instruction will become depersonalized and insensitive. If the experiment is successful, it could mean the long-term replacement of teachers with robots. In fact, many teachers fear that the agenda for the Huxley Corporation is to replace most teachers in the country with robots. (See the attached data about achievement, student enrollment, and finances at Floodrock.) The members of the Floodrock Board of Education recognize the controversial nature of the decision they are about to make, so they have established an advisory committee with representatives from the school system and from the community, including a student participant. The committee has been charged with studying the prospect of seeking a grant to purchase five robot teachers for the coming semester. Since the grants are available for a short period of time, the committee and the school board must act quickly to decide.

Question for discussion: *Should the Floodrock School Board seek a grant from the Foundation for Liberty and Prosperity to purchase five Alpha Master robot teachers to teach selected classes for the coming school term?*

Points of view: Of course, not everyone in the community agrees that it would be a good idea to try out the robot teachers on students at the high school. To deepen our understanding of the issues involved in the situation, it is useful to look at the problem from the several perspectives represented by interested parties and members of the community. What would each person have to say about the current controversy? Note the directions for group preparation and consult the available data sheets to help you formulate your arguments for your assigned character's point of view. Here are seven distinct perspectives, in addition to the role of the superintendent, who serves as the facilitator for the meeting:

- Karen (or Karl) Debs, President of the Floodrock Teachers Association (teachers' union)
- Mr. Rob (or Ms. Roberta) Ott, Sales Manager, Huxley Corporation
- Minnie (or Minden) Pinch, Business Manager, Floodrock School District 49
- Mrs. Forsythia (or Mr. Forsythe) Robinson, a parent of a student with special needs
- Chris Tenning, a "gifted" tenth-grade student
- Charlie (or Charlotte) Fairbury, a retiree
- Carla (or Carl) Hammond, community member

In addition to this case narrative and the suggested six perspectives, the university students included data sets (i.e., "facts" about the high school and specifications for the Alpha Master 84 robot teacher) and directions for a sequence of discussions. The discussions would include small group preparation in which students discussed and planned arguments their character would make in the advisory committee meeting, and a debriefing among the whole class. As the preservice teachers saw it, the sequence of discussions would engage the high school students in constructing and testing oral arguments so they could learn the procedures for analyzing the benefits and disadvantages associated with purchasing and using robot teachers. Here is the basic prompt for the subsequent writing:

> **Your Written Response to the Case**
>
> After you have heard the arguments on all sides of the question about seeking a grant to purchase robot teachers, you should have formed a conclusion about whether or not this purchase would be a good idea. The school seeks your advice. Write a letter to the school board to advise them about this question: *Should the school board accept a grant from the Foundation for Liberty and Prosperity to purchase two robot teachers to teach several classes at Floodrock High School?*

The Process of Design

The planning of an inquiry-based instructional activity to prepare students to write elaborated compositions began with attention to three important *studies,* to use Tyler's (1969) term. The planners considered what activity structures seemed to represent authentic literacy experience: that is, something that adults would do outside of the conventional tasks often imposed on learners in a school. This led to the decision to develop a problem-based activity—in this instance a case study about a debatable issue. The planners also attended to what debatable topics seemed to appeal to adolescents at particular schools—attention to what the learners seemed to *like*. The survey results revealed what high school students preferred to discuss. The designers of the activity paid attention to the procedures and content valued in their discipline, whether they were influenced by NCTE standards, Common Core State Standards, or their own amalgamated sense of what was important to know in the field of English language arts. They also had to judge whether their proposed structures to foster learning were consistent with learning theory, as they understood theory, and whether they were consistent with their philosophical values, such as developing a sense of community, living a democratic experience, or valuing divergent perspectives about debatable problems.

As with any teacher who plans new lessons, there is a stage when the planner reflects on intentions and projects the likelihood that learners will respond in an anticipated way. At the university we could go beyond individual projection, because we had a chance to test out the activity. This was not the same as testing the activity in the high school classroom, since the planners perhaps reacted the way they had wished; but the trial run in class allowed the preservice teachers to check for the clarity of directions, the distinction among points of view, and the appropriateness of the sequence of discussions for engaging participants in the procedures for argument. This inhouse test is part of what Hillocks (1995) calls "reflection in planning." Hillocks notes that "the goal of planning will be to invent materials and activities that will engage students in using specific processes and strategies relevant to particular writing tasks" (p. 125). It seemed at this point in the planning that the problem of thc robot teacher and the structures for discussing the case were likely to engage learners in processes important for argument (e.g., supporting claims, interpreting evidence, recognizing and evaluating competing points of view), which in turn would likely prepare learners for writing elaborated arguments.

Responses among Adolescent Learners

One high school teacher, whom we will refer to as Ms. Torino, who surveyed her classes about the problems they preferred to discuss, actually used the case and the instructions developed by the university methods students as a gateway into an inquiry-based unit that invited the high school students to think about their dependence on, and relationship to, technology, and their assessment of the importance of human relationships. The discussions that we observed and recorded occurred late in the spring. The teacher had already established with the students specific protocols for operating in small group activities and in large group discussions. For example, the students had come to understand that the teacher expected speakers to support their claims with relevant data, especially in the form of citations from texts, accompanied by appropriate commentary about the citation. Students also had become accustomed to practicing *uptake,* which involves offering a contribution that overtly builds on a previous speaker's comments. Uptake might be a reference to an earlier comment such as "I disagree with Mark's comments about the cost." Often, uptake involves a brief paraphrase of another's comments: "Earlier, Alyssa said that the robots can't replace teachers because teaching is a creative act that involves a teacher adjusting to students' reactions at the moment. I agree to an extent." These students were also familiar with the practice of calling on a subsequent speaker so the learners rather than the teacher facilitated the conversational turns, following a standard for involving as many speakers as possible and not letting a few speakers dominate the conversations. Many of the behaviors exhibited during discussion align with the Common Core State Standards—especially supporting claims with evidence, interpreting data, and representing and evaluating competing points of view.

In the observed high school class, the discussions about the robot teacher case proceeded in three stages. In the first phase, the teacher, Ms. Torino, organized the students into six groups, each representing a different character's perspective about the problem at the center of the case. In this initial discussion, the students formed an identity for a character who held a specific perspective, they constructed the argument that the character would make in regard to the policy question, and they anticipated how others would oppose their arguments so they would be prepared to respond. After the students had sufficient time to form their arguments, Ms. Torino organized the classroom so a set of seven desks formed a circle at the center of the classroom. One student served in the role of the school superintendent and facilitated the role-playing discussion. Students who were not enacting roles sat outside the inner circle, but were able to switch places at designated times so several students could move in and out of the "fishbowl."

The following excerpt of the simulated advisory committee discussion reveals the competing arguments.* As "Superintendent Sterling" notes, each character gets uninterrupted time to offer an argument before opening up the forum to the give and take of debate.

SUPERINTENDENT STERLING (ALIANA): The purpose of this meeting is to discuss if the school board should seek a grant to buy five Alpha Master robot teachers. We are assembled as a committee to discuss whether or not to seek the grant that would allow the purchase. Each person will have a chance to testify before we open things up for discussion and questions. ***[The student who facilitates the simulated meeting begins by setting a purpose and describing the discussion protocol.]***

KAREN DEBS, PRESIDENT OF LOCAL TEACHERS' UNION (ZETHRA): Teachers are more beneficial. If the robots replace teachers there will be a huge loss of jobs in the community. About thirty-three teachers will lose their jobs if they are replaced by robots. That would not be practical because you would create more problems in the community that is already suffering from unemployment.

*The excerpts from classroom discussions and the sample of student writing were collected with assent from students and consent from their parents, following a protocol approved by the Institutional Review Board at Northern Illinois University, DeKalb, Illinois. The names of all of the students and teachers throughout the book are pseudonyms.

[A speaker initiates the series of exchanges by arguing against the proposed change.]

CHARLIE FAIRBURY, A RETIREE (AHMED): If the teachers lose their jobs, the school board will have to pay $750,000 for each robot teacher. This cost will raise my taxes, and I don't even have kids in the school. It is just not worth it.

ROB OTT, SALESPERSON FOR THE ALPHA MASTER 84 (GLENN): I would also like to talk about the cost. The teacher's salary is about $46,000 per year. If the teacher teaches for twenty years, the robot in the long run becomes cheaper than the teacher. It will be cheaper and the company can help financially to get the project started.

[After hearing the opposition, the speaker opposes the arguments by offering a cost/benefit analysis.]

CARL HAMMOND, BUSINESS MANAGER FOR SCHOOL DISTRICT (BEN): Initially the robots are expensive, but over time, the cost will come down dramatically. In the long run, it will be cheaper for the taxpayers in the district.

FORSYTHIA ROBINSON, A PARENT OF A STUDENT WITH SPECIAL NEEDS (BRETT): Teachers have more compassion than robots. My daughter has special needs. I can see that it would be helpful to have a robot as a teaching assistant so that students with special needs can get help in each classroom. I think it will help students to move into mainstream classes, which I am interested in.

[The speaker argues for a position by making emotional and ethical appeals.]

CHRIS TENNING, A "GIFTED" STUDENT (MYUNG): I have different needs than most students. The teachers have been critical to my success throughout the years. Teachers have inspired me and helped me to discover that I can do things that I did not think I could do. The robots cannot replace human interaction.

[The speaker testifies about the effect that human teachers have had on his life and notes that his needs are distinctive.]

ROB OTT (GLENN): [referring to Ms. Robinson] You said you want them to be assistants, and you want teachers who will be sympathetic. The Alpha Masters 84 are programmed to be responsive and empathic. They can recognize human emotion and are programmed to respond empathically.

[The speaker practices **uptake** *by noting the previously stated claims and then responds to opposition.]*

CHRIS TENNING (MYUNG): The robot does not give the real feeling of being human. It is important to me to form a trusting relationship with a teacher. A robot cannot form a trusting feeling.

MS. ROBINSON (BRETT): The robot has trouble telling when people are too close to each other and doesn't understand social norms. My child is autistic and needs to learn about social norms. How will a robot teacher that doesn't feel the need for personal space be prepared to help my child in picking up social cues?

[The speaker adds a level of complication by noting a student's special needs.]

CHARLIE FAIRBURY (AHMED): As far as social interaction is concerned, when I went to school, we didn't have technology and we turned out fine and can run the country and everything. Kids today with all the technology don't know how to interact with other humans.

CARL HAMMOND (BEN): Are you saying that our children should not have access to the latest technology? In society, technology is part of our daily lives.

This is just a portion of a longer exchange. In fact, the students sustained the discussion for forty minutes without the teacher's intervention. While one representative from each group (i.e., each character) began the discussion, some students switched places with their group partners as the discussion continued. But even this small portion illustrates several procedures in action: Superintendent Sterling summarizes the problem, prompts the contributions, and manages the order of the speakers. Often the speakers begin by referencing a previous speaker (i.e., practicing *uptake*): e.g., "you said you want them to be assistants, and you want teachers who will be sympathetic." These references provide the context for the contribution and link comments together. The speakers acknowledge and evaluate the previous positions as they advance their own arguments for or against a policy proposition regarding the efficacy of investment in the robot teachers.

Classes probably could jump directly into the discussion about the use of robot teachers without this initial role-playing element, but we have found that the role-playing stage has an important function because it situates students to acknowledge the many ways to look at the question. We find students arguing the issue on several grounds: financial, emotional, ethical, and practical. The role-playing positions that students have articulated serve as texts, from which all students can draw information and testimonials. The resulting arguments are nuanced, recognizing that for some students the personal relationship with the teacher is crucial, while for others, the problem is purely financial, devoid of emotional dimensions. The role-playing speakers ask for attention to the fiscal well-being of the school district, to the efficacy of the robot's instruction, to various learners' emotional and social needs, and to loyal employees who might soon be out of work. As the discussion continues, and later when students prepare to write a response, they evaluate the arguments they have heard: Some they reject, some they contrast with their own views, some they embrace, and some they combine or qualify.

In the next stage, in another class meeting, Ms. Torino asked students to cast off their assigned characters and argue from their own personal perspectives. She formed the whole class into a circle and called on a volunteer to begin the discussion. The first speaker then called on the next speaker; and this process continued, with no teacher interruption, for forty-two minutes. Here is a segment of this extensive discussion:

KARUNA: It [using robot teachers] is trying to fix something that doesn't need to be fixed. There are imperfections and that is a good thing. . . . And the idea of being available 24/7, I am not sure that is a good thing. . . . You are taught to respond in only a certain way.

PETER: I think we are drifting away from the original topic of the discussion. There are only five robot teachers and there are ninety teachers. There are still other human teachers. It is to try things out. It is like an online course at our high school. It is not taking over the whole school. Like in math, I don't think you need to be taught in a human way. . . .

LANI: They are thinking about if the pilot works out, they would expand the use of robots. One programmed response would not meet everyone's needs. Sometimes I struggle with math and I need a human teacher to help.

GREG: I think that once we decide to use robot teachers [refers to Vonnegut's "The Veldt"], we will allow technology to manage our lives.

MICHAEL: It is inevitable that we are going to deal more and more with technology . . . if you . . .

SASHA: At the Floodrock school, students are still going to have interactions with other students. But in this case, with achievement dropping . . .

ALIANA: In the end, robots could be detrimental [cites *New York Times* article]. Kids will be able to find ways to cheat the system. In certain subjects, you can always find ways to cheat the system. It will be really detrimental. Kids will learn to dishonestly get by.

LAURA: It says in the *New York Times* article, the e-reader doesn't like short sentences and short paragraphs. . . .

[Throughout the exchange, the students cite outside sources, including fiction that serves as a warning and current newspaper articles.]

LANI: You are just doing what the robot wants you to do instead of doing something productive.

STEPHANIE: Can we outsmart the robots? Do we know more than they do?

ABBY: It is only as smart as the person who programs it.

SASHA: In the system as it is, it is unfair, like in English or language class. Different teachers grade in different ways. The robots are programmed to teach the same way with each student in each class. We hear kids complain about this teacher doesn't like me and gives me bad grades. That is another advantage.

[The speaker argues from an ethical principle—that teachers need to be fair, objective, and consistent in their grading.]

ALIANA: I agree with the grading part, but for me when I struggled with math, the teacher had only this one way and would not stray. We are so impatient, like we are texting, we want immediate response. While it is annoying to email our teacher and not get a response, that's normal. While grading is unfair, there isn't just one path.

[The speaker begins by referring to the previous comment, which sets the context for her new observation.]

BEN: When would it be ethical to fire teachers to replace them with technology?

LAURA: This happens all the time, like during the Industrial Revolution. New methods and inventions will cause the loss of jobs.

FARRELL: I am going back to Stephanie's question and Abby's response. You could cheat the system. If we discover the patterns, we could put them to work for us. In the real world with bosses and things, we won't have robot bosses and you won't always have people treating everyone the same way.

[The speaker contextualizes his comment by referring to an earlier exchange between two classmates and extends the discussion by noting a new principle—that school should prepare learners for future experiences.]

In the two observed class meetings, the students did almost all of the talking and sustained their attention to the issue at hand, even with one student reminding the class when they seemed to drift from the central question. The transcripts reveal that the students were able to summarize the problem and take a position relative to the central question. The students repeatedly referred to the arguments of others and evaluated those arguments. Students advanced their own arguments in the context of the broader conversation about our relationship to technology. In constructing their arguments, the students cited and interpreted both "informational" and literary texts. These procedures—summarize, analyze, synthesize, argue, cite, interpret, and evaluate—align with the prompt that directs the students to write about the case and reflect the CCSS for writing argument and analysis.

The transcripts of the extensive discussions reveal that students are active, both as speakers and listeners, in practicing the procedures that are important for producing an academic essay. The work of thc high school teacher and the university methods students involved an analysis of the writing task, an assessment of who the students were and what drew their interest, and the creation of learning activities that engaged and sustained students over several days. From reading the transcripts of the discussions and the essays, it was clear to us that the students learned much. But from observing the classes, it was also apparent that the students were enjoying themselves—enjoying the playful seriousness of assuming a character identity and simulating an advisory committee meeting, enjoying the bit of competition of ideas, and imagining their own school and their own lives with robots managing their learning. Many students left the classroom still talking about the prospect of robot teachers, and the learners had extensive notes from the several exchanges about the issue, positioning them to be able to write elaborated essays. The following composition is representative of the essays submitted in two classes. The essay reveals the effect and critical importance of the discussions that preceded the writing, as we discuss below.

Sample Composition

Lea Aloue

The school board of Floodrock High is faced with the decision of allowing or not allowing robot teachers to begin teaching classes with a grant from the Foundation for Liberty and Prosperity. While some believe that the new technology would establish new and up-to-date ways of teaching and cut costs of teacher salaries, others are concerned about the overexposure of technology and the loss of jobs. Robots have the potential to help students at all levels to learn more efficiently, but limitations exist on the skills that programs can assess, so the amount of robots in the classroom should be limited to what the grant provides.

Robots have capabilities that would assist students, particularly students with special needs, to learn better and faster. Based on research, robots can be programmed to help keep students focused and alert. Through experiments, it was determined that "students given a cue by the robot when their attention was waning were much better at recalling" information presented (*New Scientist*). Since these robots can detect when a students becomes disengaged through precise sensors, it can be presumed that robots will be able to bring the student's focus back and offers a good alternative to human teachers who may not always sense when a student is not focused. Additionally, technology can do what teachers could do faster as well. An automated reader called an e-reader "can grade 16,000 essays in 20 seconds" (*NY Times*), much faster than a human ever could. The technology allows students to receive feedback much quicker and therefore could get through more material quicker. Robots are also an asset to students with special needs, as shown by robots already implemented in special needs classrooms. Kossyraki states that "there are no subtle non-verbal behaviors to confuse them" (*Telegraph*) because students with a disorder like autism often have difficulties with social interaction. Robots allow for them to first practice interacting with something simpler, then moving on to [interactions] with real people. Mrs. Forsythia, a parent with a student with special needs at Floodrock High School, stated that she had "high hopes for robots in the classroom" (transcript) due to previous studies that have proven the effectiveness of robots teaching autistic students. Due to the benefits and increased efficiency that robots can teach both regular and autistic students, robots are a valuable asset in the classroom.

While robots improve efficiency, they still have limitations on what they can teach because everything is programmed into them and they are unable to independently adapt. Robots do not allow for personalized teaching because of their limited skill set. Robots are constrained to the clearly defined curriculum "not because they are the most important, but because true pattern-matching is easier to program" (*New Yorker*). Because robots can only teach what they are programmed, they cannot teach in a flexible way that accounts for potential questions students have. The limitations are exemplified by essay grading programs which are more geared toward analyzing technicalities rather than content. As Les Perelman, director of writing at MIT stated, the facts in the essay don't matter "as long as it looks to the computer as if it's nicely argued" (*NY Times*). The program views grammatical content as more important than factual content and therefore only helps students in a limited way. The concern is expressed by an honors student at Floodrock High School who spoke that they were worried they "would not be able to learn advanced topics because of the robot's limited capabilities" (transcript). Because robots are confined to what they are programmed, harder and more abstract topics could pose a challenge and make teaching less effective. While in some aspects robots can be faster, the limited capabilities by its coding make teaching less straight-forward and classes less effective.

Robots present a promising new alternative, but teachers are still a much needed asset in the classroom. A teacher in a classroom which has already imple-

> mented robot teachers stated that "at one point, teachers had to guard against this bond" the student had with its robot because it was too strong (*Telegraph*). Exposing students to such direct contact with robots runs the risk of developing unhealthy relationships with a machine that has no emotions. While robots can be an aid in teaching, the emotional connection must still be established with a human teacher. Therefore, robots and humans must share the responsibilities in the classroom because compassion is still needed for effective teaching. Mr. Watersworth, the head of school at a UK school, proposes that robots can record interactions with students and if any abnormalities are detected, "then the teacher can make an interaction" (*Telegraph*). By doing so, robots are used more as a tool, allowing for teachers to intervene in emotional issues so the factor of compassion is still present. Limiting the number of robots at Floodrock High School would also prevent teachers from losing jobs. The president of the Teachers' Union stated that they were "concerned that robots would take away jobs" (transcript), considering that each [robot] costs $700,000 (specifications from Alpha Master 84).

Lea's essay reveals the transfer of classroom deliberation procedures to her writing. The writer accurately frames the problem the class has considered and has expressed a balanced stand about the question. This involves *summary* and *evaluation*, which students practiced to introduce the discussion and to refer to other speakers as they contextualized their comments during the many classroom interchanges. The writer *connects* several arguments, drawing from the texts accessed online as part of their preparation for, and extension of, discussion (e.g., articles from the *New York Times*, the *New Yorker*, the *New Scientist*, and the *Telegraph*) and *citing* and *interpreting* the testimonies from the simulated meeting. Lea refers to the characters by name and appropriately *quotes their testimony* as instances of experience, expressions of concern or need, and attention to issues that could impact decisions. This development in the essay involves the interpretation of the texts cited. It also requires *attention to various opinions*, which allows the writer to arrive at a balanced response to the problem.

The simulated meeting of an advisory committee not only allowed students to hear competing views, but the collision of ideas actually seems to have shaped the student's thinking. The student quotes the testimonies—e.g., the parent of the student with special needs, the gifted learner. Without the simulated meeting, the student would not have these sources of support. The testimonies are not reports of documented "facts" about the case; the quotes from the discussants offer examples of the potential impact of human teachers and robot teachers. Even though the people testifying are not actual authorities, their personal examples seem to be realistic possibilities and illustrate the potential effect of the decision to use robot teachers. Considering the way the enacted meeting helped to shape the students' thinking about the issue and provided testimonies that could be incorporated into a written response, much would be lost by skipping the simulation step.

During the course of the school year, Ms. Torino had been preparing the learners to follow the protocols necessary for civil and rational discourse, as demonstrated in the discussion represented above. This preparation is a long-term process that will vary from teacher to teacher, as we discuss in some detail in Chapter 4. The sequence leading to the elaborated written responses involved three big steps—preparing for the roles, participating in the simulated meeting, and debriefing about personal responses to the problem. Each step prepared the discussants for the next step. In a sense, the dialogue proceeded in layers, with each layer serving a function to help the students think critically about the central question and write an elaborated response (cf. VanDerHeide & Newell, 2013; Newell, Bloome, & Hirvela, 2015). The student's composition, in connection with the discussion transcripts, as well as the writing of other students in the class, shows clearly that students learn to write—at least in part—by talking. The wide participation and the extensive contributions suggest that the students find the talk highly engaging.

In designing a scaffolded series of discussions, the preservice teachers and Ms. Torino recognized the purpose for each step in the process and provided opportunities for the learners to work with the procedures that would be important for a complex written analysis. As the discussion excerpts above illustrate, as students talked to each other, they explored the problem, developed preliminary arguments,

The practices in Ms. Torino's class immersed students in significant literacy procedures while the learning activities honored elements important to adolescents.

Honoring Student Choice

While the teacher did not allow students' complete autonomy, she sought to learn what interested students and what was likely to invest them in extended inquiry. While the teacher selected texts that would support inquiry, she designed the inquiry around the focus that students had selected.

Affirming Student Competency

When discussion is indeed ***authentic***, the teacher has framed a problem for which every student can feel equally competent in contributing insights and recommendations. In the discussions about the proposed purchase of robot teachers, no learner was more expert than others. The designed preparation and the open-ended nature of the central questions allowed each student to feel like a competent contributor to the deliberations that could influence a school board's decision.

Fostering Student Interaction

Ms. Torino judged that a genuinely debatable problem was likely to prompt discussions, but she also knew that the general tone of the classroom, the choices for group membership, and the protocols for engaging in conversations all contributed to students' willingness to join in. While the students inevitably disagreed with each other as part of the process of problem-solving, they were not engaged in competitive debate; instead, they joined in collaborative deliberations, trusting that no classmate would challenge them in a way that was hurtful or demeaning. The wide participation was the product of a safe and supportive environment, a genuine student-selected problem as the focus of inquiry, and an affirmation that every class member had something to contribute.

summarized the case, paraphrased the arguments of others, evaluated several competing arguments, drew from several sources to make decisions and support claims, recognized the merits of alternative arguments, and connected several arguments together. These steps and procedures are key to inquiry: defining a problem, accessing and evaluating data, deliberating with others to assess the merits of various responses or courses of action, and advancing an argument for a specific policy in the context of the broad conversation about what action to take.

Creating and Extending a Circle of Experience and Delight

The sequence for planning and facilitating instruction reveals much about the kind of experiences that students find engaging. To extend this inquiry even further, teachers could build upon this sequence of activities, using it as an introduction into *a consistent line of inquiry in a coherent unit* where students would read additional texts dealing with issues of technology in our lives, including news articles, opinion pieces, poems, fiction narratives, and film, viewing these texts through a critical lens, and connecting the information, opinions, and implications offered in the texts. Students would be invited to think further about their relationship to, and reliance on, technology. As part of this inquiry, the students would be thinking about the importance of human relationships, an issue the preliminary survey revealed as appealing to the learners.

Perhaps honoring students' choice of topic also fostered engagement. The choice guided the preservice teachers in designing the sequence of experiences and in making related texts available to the learners. The student-directed, sustained discussions and the subsequent elaborated compositions suggest that the students enjoyed what they were doing. Their delight came from grappling with others in tackling an everyday problem that all the participants felt equally capable of solving. Peers worked with each other; affirmed their competence as discussants, readers, and writers; and saw their choice of topics honored. Part of the sequence involved learners at play—role-playing in an imagined adult forum, which the students executed with good humor and civility. The whole sequence—survey to development to enactment—represents a circle of experience, one in which the high school students learned generative procedures that can apply to many occasions, and the university preservice teachers learned details about planning instruction and witnessing the effect of instruction. We judge that for everyone involved, the sequence of experiences taught the participants a lot, and delighted them in the process.

As we have learned from observing in a variety of schools, the teachers who involved students in extensive discussions about significant contemporary problems attended to three important considerations: (1) What problem or concept is likely to foster students' commitment to reading, discussing, and writing? This consideration honors students' judgments about consequential matters. (2) How can the discussion forums affirm students' competencies in evaluating data and judging the potential efficacy of proposed actions? The teachers' efforts allowed students to showcase what they knew, rather than emphasizing what they didn't know. (3) How can students engage with their peers in conversations that encourage participation and protect the dignity of everyone involved? In Ms. Torino's class, as students talked extensively over three class meetings, they repeatedly practiced procedures of analysis and argument; at the same time, they appeared to appreciate that the teacher honored their choice of an inquiry focus, they felt competent in what they were doing, and they had extended opportunities to talk to peers.

3 Teachers and Students in Action: Factors That Account for Engagement and Production

In Chapter 2, we shared some of the discussion and writing from Ms. Torino's class. We noted that we observed one of her tenth-grade classes as students deliberated about the prospect of a school district investing in robot teachers, a topic that the students chose to discuss. When the students played the roles of the stakeholders in the case, they facilitated the discussion themselves and sustained the discussion for forty minutes without the teacher's intervention. In a subsequent class meeting, the students discussed the proposal again from their own points of view and sustained the discussion, with no teacher voice, for forty-two minutes. As teachers who have had a long history of teaching English in high schools and facilitating many discussions, from fifth grade through college, we find these numbers noteworthy, if not astonishing. We also wondered how to account for the phenomena that we observed.

As a basis for comparison, the ninth graders in the Nystrand (1997) study engaged in authentic discussion, on average, for 15 seconds per class meeting. In contrast, in Ms. Torino's class, the students engaged in discussion during one observation for 2,400 seconds, or 160 times the average in the Nystrand study. On the second day, students discussed for 2,520 seconds, or 168 times the average in the Nystrand study. Of course, one could wonder if these two classes were an aberration and students were more passive during the rest of the school year. Consider, however, that if Ms. Torino's class never said another word for the other 178 days of the school year, their average engagement in authentic discussion would still be 27 seconds per day, or almost twice the average from the Nystrand study!

We certainly hope that the typical patterns of discourse have changed dramatically since the Nystrand 1997 study, but Nystrand's 2017 report reveals that Ms. Torino's class remains an exception. Not only have we noted the amount of time engaged in discussion, but we also examined the transcripts to see what occurred during discussion. We trained three graduate students to code the transcripts to reveal patterns of students' interchanges. The results of this coding across two class meetings are also revealing: no instances of students socializing, 56 instances of students practicing uptake, 115 instances of students support-

Table 3.1. Summary of Discussion Behaviors in Ms.Torino's Class

Numbers and percentages for discussion moves	Simulated Meeting	Whole Class Discussion
Number of seconds in authentic discussion	2,400	2,520
Number of instances of social conversation	0	0
Percentage of time students are speaking	96.4	98.6
Number of interruptions of peers speaking	2	1
Number of instances of citing data	69	46
Number of instances of citing warrants	28	55
Number of instances of students practicing uptake	20	36
Number of words per conversational turn	48.6	111

ing claims with relevant data, 83 instances of applying warrants to interpret data, and no instances of students responding to each other in a disrespectful way. Across the observations in two class meetings, all students actively participated in the discussions in some form—through small group work, during role-playing, and through whole class deliberation. Perhaps most impressive is the extent of each participant's contribution to the deliberation: 48 words per conversational turn on the first day of observations and 111 words per conversational turn on the second day. Table 3.1 provides a summary of the tallying and coding for the two observed discussions.

Rare Exception or Mark of Potential?

We observed Ms. Torino's classes and envied her for having students participate as enthusiastically and extensively as they did. As university faculty charged with preparing future middle school and high school English teachers, we recognize a need to know how Ms. Torino accomplished such an astounding classroom experience. If we can understand the factors that account for the students' performance, we can reveal to our preservice teachers or to more experienced teachers how such discussions occur, and far more students will be able to experience what the students in Ms. Torino's class experienced. As a result, far more students would be able to enjoy the experience of engaging in dialogue with their peers about issues of consequence and in the process learn important literacy procedures, including supporting claims, interpreting data, connecting and evaluating a set of competing arguments, listening actively and critically to the arguments of others, building on the contributions of speakers to refine and extend arguments, and judging the merits of a policy by measuring its costs and impact on various stakeholders. In Ms. Torino's example, we saw also that students were able to connect the discussions about a contemporary problem to their interpretation and assessment of literary texts as part of a program of shared inquiry, as we discuss in Chapter 6.

We return to the four possible factors that we have identified to account for the extensive discussion participation in Ms. Torino's class: (1) Is it simply a matter that her students are a special group, predisposed to want to participate in discussions? Was Ms. Torino just fortunate enough to have a class full of cooperative, bright, and enthusiastic students? (2) Is it the case that Ms. Torino is an especially gifted and charismatic teacher? Is it the case that one has to have a certain kind of personality or charisma to influence students to participate widely and extensively in authentic discussion? (3) Was it the topic itself, and the fact that students selected the topic themselves, that accounts for the kind of discussions we witnessed? If this were the case, we would have to know what kind of problems particularly resonate with adolescents. (4) Was it the structure or design of the discussion activities that made the difference? Certainly students had time for preparation, and there were three distinct and scaffolded stages, which would, theoretically, encourage participation.

So, we have sought to understand how these factors—students, teacher, instructional design, topic—affect the classroom discourse. Although it is hard to quantify the impact of each factor and its relative effects, our immediate conclusion is that most likely all of these factors influence what happens in the classroom. We recruited other teachers to engage their students in gateway activities similar to the Robot Teacher activity and to allow us to observe in their classrooms. As we hope to make evident in the following analysis and discussion, our observations reveal to us that almost any teacher with any class in any school can engage students in extensive and connected discussions about issues that learners find meaningful.

Discovering a Resonant Problem

We expanded the process of learning what students, as a group, most wanted to discuss. Scanning the pages of newspapers and listening to radio and television news programs, we identified fourteen stories that seemed likely to interest adolescents. Our years of experience in teaching in high schools allowed us to pick issues that seemed to resonate with teens—e.g., problems with friendship and romance, conflicts about parental control and need for freedom, issues with fairness and justice, and tensions between respect for authority and a need to protect personal interests and values. As we had done with earlier classes, we wanted to present students with very brief narratives about the problems; but we recognized that a survey that contained fourteen narrative representations could be overwhelming for the reader. In the end, the survey responses would not be very revealing if some students quit attending to the descriptions toward the end of the survey. To reduce the length of the survey, we asked ten high school English teachers to scan the fourteen problems and advise us about which were most likely to appeal to the students in their classes. The responses from the ten teachers allowed us to reduce the choices to eight contemporary problems. We have attached the complete survey as Appendix A, but we offer here the descriptions of two choices that the teachers judged as especially appealing to their students:

> **Examining "White Privilege":** In a high school social studies class, a unit on diversity included lessons on "white privilege." A definition was given to students stating that in critical race theory, *white privilege* is a set of advantages that are believed to be enjoyed by white people beyond those commonly experienced by nonwhite people in the same social, political, and economic spaces (nation, community, workplace, income, etc.). In other words, it provides white people with "perks" that they do not earn and that people of color do not enjoy. For example, if I am a white person, when I am in a store, I don't have to worry about security personnel watching me closely or following me because of my skin color. In class, students were engaged in discussing their views about the existence of "white privilege" and its possible effects. Some parents in the community objected to the lessons, arguing that they were teaching white students that they should feel guilty and creating division and conflict among students. They questioned why the school would do something that could destroy the peace and goodwill among all races in the community. Should the school eliminate the lessons on "white privilege" and any discussion of the issue? Do lessons like this decrease or increase racial tensions and conflicts? Can a teacher decide independently to teach such lessons?

> **Wazzup!** A social media app called "Wazzup!" allows contributors within a limited range (e.g., within twenty miles of a college campus) to post messages on a continuous feed. Students on college campuses use the app to share where parties are happening, where drugs are available, and how they got wasted recently. Parents of high school seniors have tapped into this feed to gain insight into the social environment of the colleges where their sons or daughters have applied for admission. Many students see the parents have misrepresented themselves as students and have intruded into the private world of the life on the college

campuses. For their part, college and university professors have been appalled by what they have seen on "Wazzup!" They fret that parents and potential students will get the wrong idea about their institutions by depending on the incoherent postings by a relative few drug-addled and alcohol-soaked undergraduates. Some more proactive professors have started to post their own messages about upcoming lectures, art exhibits, concerts, plays, poetry readings, and other elements of the cultural and intellectual life of the campuses. These professors hope that their counter-narrative will leave a more positive impression on parents. Many high school seniors would like to see their parents and the college professors remove themselves from the "Wazzup!" exchanges, noting that their intrusions are both dishonest and inappropriate.

Seven of the ten teachers were able to survey their classes. The respondents included students from rural schools, urban schools, and suburban schools. All together, 401 students, including respondents from grades 9, 10, 11, and 12, completed the survey. We offer a summary of the survey results in two forms: Table 3.2 shows a summary of the trends across the combined responses; Table 3.3 provides a summary by school location (i.e., rural/small town, suburban, and urban).

Table 3.2. Summary of Survey Responses across Seven Schools

All Schools		
Case	**Mean**	**SD**
Fighting: Should a school change its mascot and school fight song so as not to glorify fighting?	2.06	0.87
Robot Teacher: Should a high school invest in the use of robot teachers?	2.63	1.00
Wazzup! Should parents and professors have access to a social media application?	2.74	1.02
Boys Cry: Should a youth hockey league direct a coach from an aggressive approach to winning?	2.47	1.02
White Privilege: Should a high school include the teaching of the concept of *white privilege* in its social studies curriculum?	2.84	1.03
Fall in Love: Should a high school student follow a behavior modification protocol to "make" a peer fall in love?	2.70	1.02
Lynching: Should the more than 800 lynching sites in the United States be marked with commemorative plaques?	2.45	1.01
Character: Should an inclusive and supportive youth baseball coach step down in favor of someone more focused on winning?	2.54	1.02

Table 3.3. Summary of Survey Responses by School Location (Rural/Small Town, Suburban, and Urban)

	Rural		Suburban		Urban	
Case	**Mean**	**SD**	**Mean**	**SD**	**Mean**	**SD**
Fighting	2.67	0.99	1.86	0.79	2.18	0.85
Robot	2.54	0.96	2.69	0.98	2.57	1.07
Wazzup!	2.87	1.05	2.81	0.99	2.58	1.06
Boys Cry	2.48	1.07	2.45	0.99	2.50	1.05
White Privilege	2.63	0.97	2.76	1.05	3.05	0.98
Fall in Love	2.57	1.09	2.58	1.03	2.95	0.92
Lynching	2.52	1.01	2.29	0.99	2.71	0.99
Character	2.63	1.10	2.53	1.04	2.53	0.95

Our interest in discovering what students would like to talk about was not a mere pandering to students' tastes and preferences. We judged that if teachers were going to immerse students in the kind of conversations that would challenge learners to think critically and practice several important literacy procedures (synthesizing arguments, supporting claims, interpreting support, responding to challenges, etc.), then the subjects at the heart of those conversations would have to be issues that students cared about. We wanted to imbue with purpose the effort to read a variety of texts, talk extensively with peers, and write thoroughly about problems.

It would appear, then, that the controversy about teaching the concept of white privilege would be of most interest to the students (Figure 3.1). More accurately, however, the survey results reveal that students appeared interested in discussing at least seven out of the eight problems. In fact, an analysis of the data shows that while there was a difference across the set of problems ($F = 23.236$; $p < .0001$), only one of the choices ("Stop All the Fighting") was significantly less popular than the other choices. As teachers who have long presumed to guess what topics or themes adolescents would care to explore, the results suggested to us that any one of the top seven choices would prompt considerable discussion. We chose then to develop the case about teaching the concept of white privilege.

It made sense to us to focus on developing the Teaching about White Privilege case for several reasons, including these: (1) It would allow us to see if a potentially provocative case would prompt different kinds of discussions in different classes, based on the different characteristics of the classes and/or schools. (2) We saw that the case connected with several social justice issues that

Figure 3.1. Mean responses to survey of topic interests.

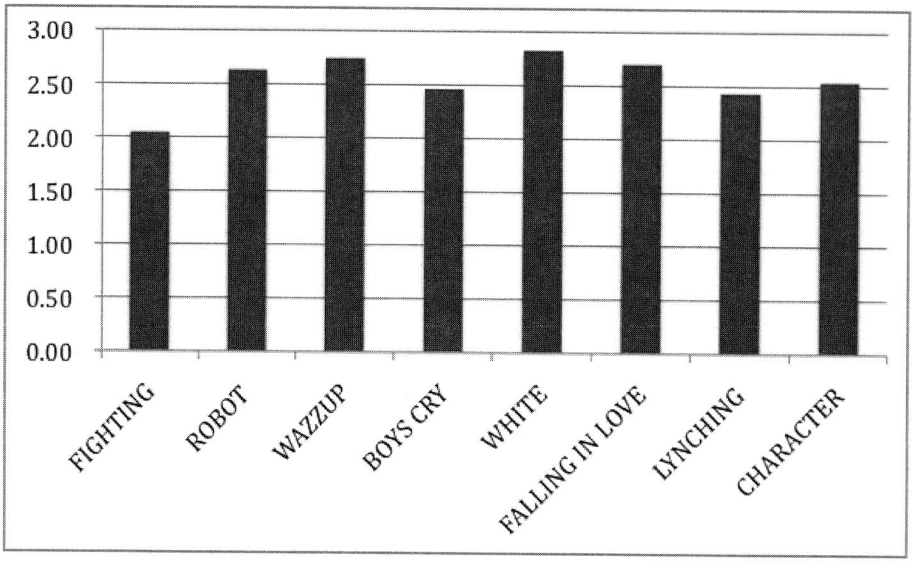

teachers saw value in studying. (3) The case could connect with a body of literature already taught in the schools: e.g., literature about issues of social justice, prejudice and bigotry, identity, and the American dream.

As we did with the Robot Teacher case that we discuss in Chapter 2, we introduced to preservice teachers the basic problem of teaching the concept of white privilege and guided them in developing the full case, including a more elaborate narrative, data sets to support thinking about the case, descriptions of the roles for multiple stakeholders, directions for stages of discussion, and directions for writing. Our university students worked in teams to develop specific components of the case. All students contributed to identifying related reading, both to support the construction of arguments and to extend the thinking about the issues in the case. The basic elements of the case appear below. A more detailed case narrative appears in Appendix B.

Teaching about "White Privilege" in High School Classes

In eleventh-grade social studies classes at Robert A. Millikan High School, a unit on diversity includes lessons on "white privilege." Teachers assign students related readings and engage learners in discussing their views about the existence of white privilege and its possible effects.

Some skepticism: Some parents have objected to the lessons, arguing that they were teaching white students that they should feel guilty. The same parents claim that the discussions about white privilege create divisions and conflicts among students. The concerned parents question why the school would do something that could destroy the peace and goodwill among all races in the community. The objecting parents have organized and have demanded that the school board reevaluate the value and efficacy of the diversity curriculum that promulgates the concept of white privilege as an established fact.

Questions for Discussion: *Should the school board support the teaching of a diversity curriculum at Millikan High School that includes attention to the concept of white privilege?*

- For someone outside the community, how would you summarize what the controversy is about?
- What harm, if any, can come from teaching students about the concept of white privilege?
- Are the lessons that focus on the concept of white privilege likely to decrease or increase racial tensions and conflicts? What is the basis for your judgment?
- On what grounds can anyone justify the elimination of the lessons on white privilege and any discussion of the issue?
- How is it possible to continue to teach a diversity curriculum without attention to the concept of white privilege?
- To what extent can the concept of white privilege be taught as an established fact?
- What do the teachers who teach the diversity curriculum see as the advantages to teaching eleventh graders about the concept of white privilege?
- Can a teacher decide independently to teach such lessons?
- On balance, are there more benefits than disadvantages to teaching high school juniors about the concept of white privilege?

Planning and Facilitating a "District Forum"

Following the small group preparation, a community meeting (District Forum) allows the various stakeholders to discuss whether Millikan High School should include instruction on the concept of white privilege in eleventh-grade social studies classes. This forum allows for students' exposure to several viewpoints (see the "Role-Playing" portion of Appendix B).

The preservice teachers specified eight roles for the stakeholders who would be involved in the superintendent's District Forum. They provided basic information about the demographics of the school and community, about the concept of white privilege, and about the ways the concept of white privilege was addressed in the social studies classes. They also identified links to related articles and videos, both to help learners understand the concept and to provide the data that would support the construction of arguments. After drafting the full case, the preservice teachers piloted it in their classes, testing the activity to determine that the directions were clear, the roles were viable, and the links were indeed useful.

Discussing White Privilege across Schools

When the final version of the Teaching about White Privilege case was available, we provided it to the high school teachers who had helped us with the survey. Four of the seven high school English teachers who had surveyed their classes decided that the discussion of the case would have a proper place in their curriculum and they planned to use it with at least one class. This sample of classes included one in a small town, two in suburbs, and one in a city. Each class had between twenty-five and thirty students, and in no class observed were there fewer than twenty-five students present. Tables 3.4 and 3.5 list the teachers and schools, using pseudonyms for each.

Table 3.4. Demographics for Participant Schools

School	Location	Enrollment	Low Income	African American	Latinx	Asian	White	Other/Two or More
Kleindorf	rural/small town	1,243	63.7%	23.7%	8.7%	1.1%	55.2%	11.3%
Mountbank	suburban	1,859	45.6%	4.9%	19.4%	32.8%	40.5%	2.4%
Stonebridge	urban	2,053	79.3%	45.5%	15.3%	3.9%	29.9%	6.1%
Nielson	suburban	2,593	32.2%	5.9%	14%	30.4%	49.2%	0.5%

Table 3.5. Grades and Levels for Participant Classes

Teacher	School	Location	Grade	Level	Teaching Experience
Ms. Brezel	Kleindorf	rural/small town	11	Honors	2 years
Mr. Damon	Mountbank	suburban	10	Regular, "Mixed Ability"	19 years
Ms. Widerhaken	Stonebridge	urban	10	Honors	10 years
Ms. Zorba	Nielson	suburban	10	Regular, "Mixed Ability"	31 years

Discussions and Observations

We observed the four high school English teachers as they engaged students in a sequence of discussions about teaching the concept of *white privilege*. Like the Robot Teacher case, the design of the Teaching about White Privilege case activity provides for three stages of discussion: a small group preparatory stage, a simulated meeting, and a whole class debriefing. We were able to observe and audio record the discussions in each class for the last two stages in the sequence. So we were able to observe and record students as they represented the arguments from several characters' points of view and as they considered the competing arguments and argued for a policy from their own points of view. A research assistant transcribed the recordings, which we edited with the help of our observation notes and the feedback from the teachers when we had questions. We trained two graduate students in English to code the transcripts. After checks during practice sessions established a high rate of reliability (90 percent agreement overall), the readers continued with the coding, with reliability checks periodically to ensure that consistency was maintained (85, 90, and 92 percent agreement). The coding system appears as Appendix C. The coding results and simple word counts appear in Table 3.6.

The results of observations (Table 3.6) reveal that all of the classes, "regular" or "honors," small town, suburban, or urban, engaged extensively in authentic discussions. In each of the classes, students accounted for more than 50 percent of the talk. Seldom did students' talk digress into social conversation. Rarely did students interrupt each other while speaking. And the number of words per conversational turn suggests that the students were not simply reciting brief comments to satisfy the teacher but were offering supported conclusions, reactions, analyses, challenges, and exceptions.

Not only did many students participate extensively, but the contributions were by and large substantive. The coding indicates that the students supported

Table 3.6. Summary of Discussion Behaviors in Classes across Four Schools

	Kleindorf H.S.		**Mountbank H.S**		**Stonebridge H.S.**		**Nielson H.S.**	
Numbers and percentages for discussion moves	Simulated Meeting	Whole Class Discussion	Simulated Meeting	Whole Class Discussion	Simulated Meeting	Whole Class Discussion	Simulated Meeting	Whole Class Discussion
Number of seconds in authentic discussion	1699	1987	1636	1448	1611	1739	1294	1509
Number of instances of social conversation	4	19	2	0	0	1	0	0
Percentage of time students are speaking	59.00	69.00	60.61	53.64	53.70	57.98	51.35	59.89
Number of interruptions of peers speaking	0	35	48	32	1	4	1	20
Number of instances of citing data	18	11	23	30	25	25	35	22
Number of instances of citing warrants	4	2	13	8	11	8	9	6
Number of instances of students practicing uptake	1	1	1	3	3	5	3	10
Number of words per conversational turn	27	16	48	32	48	51	85	38

their claims by citing data from several sources—texts, testimonials, and personal experience. Not only did students cite data, but they also interpreted these data, as indicated by the number of instances when students cited warrants (i.e., principles, rules, general tendencies).

These data, representing our observations in classes across four schools, encourage us that students in almost any context can engage productively in extensive discussions that the learners find meaningful. The coding alone reveals that in circumstances that foster extensive and connected discussions, all students are able to rely on their interactions with peers as opportunities to develop and practice important literacy procedures—especially attending to and evaluating the arguments of others and advancing their own arguments. Given the "special place" for argument in the Common Core State Standards and the importance of skills in interpreting the arguments of others and constructing arguments as part of college and career readiness, *teachers would be doing students a grave disservice if they were to assume that the learners were incapable of participating civilly and rationally in authentic discussion and to limit instruction to recitation, note-taking, and quiet, controlled seatwork.*

So, one simple takeaway for us is that students across grades, levels, and schools *can* engage in authentic discussion, even when discussion focuses on a controversial issue. Although it is possible that students were performing for an observer who was visiting the class, experience tells us that it is more likely that students would be more reluctant to speak when an unfamiliar visitor is present. While we saw students across schools engaged in authentic discussion, the participation and the substance of that participation were not a matter of chance, as if the teachers happened to have only gifted learners who were ready and willing to talk about substantive issues in their class. Through our observations, we concluded that the discussions that were observed were the result of the teachers' knowing who the learners were, adjusting an instructional plan to meet their needs and interests, establishing protocols for classroom operations, and following a carefully scaffolded sequence to support discussions and connect them. We discuss these factors in some detail below, with illustrations from the discussion transcripts.

The Student Factor

In the case of Ms. Torino, it was not that she had been blessed with an especially enthusiastic and compliant group of students, rarely to be seen in most schools. We see from the observations in classes at other schools (Table 3.6) that students in a variety of contexts are prepared to engage in extensive discussions about critical issues. To this extent, the students obviously matter, but they are not the crucial factor. Tom taught for seven years in an alternative school with students who had been dropped from enrollment at the conventional high school program. Although some teachers and administrators largely dismissed the students in the alternative school as incorrigible and uncooperative, they readily engaged in discussion about matters that they thought were significant to them and the community where they lived. So, for the teacher who is seeking wide and enthusiastic participation in discussions in English class from day to day, it is not a matter of the sectioning lottery lining up in the teacher's favor, bestowing the most highly regarded pupils in the school. But as a critical factor, students always do matter, in the sense that the teacher needs to be aware of who the learners are, how they prefer to engage in discussions that matter to them, and how their knowledge, language, and preferences need to be regarded.

Across the five classrooms, with five different teachers (including Ms. Torino) whom we observed, students contributed extensively to the daily discourse.

Students in all classes were able to express reasonable arguments by citing and interpreting data. At the same time, we see differences, with one class more inclined to social conversation than the others, and students in four classes less inclined than the students in Ms. Torino's class to practice uptake. In some cases across the four classes, students had been absent and were not prepared for the discussions when they returned to class. These situations required the teacher's flexibility and adaptation in regard to pacing, grouping, and structuring the discussion forums. As we discuss in detail in Chapter 5, these distinctions require attention to who the students are; but judgments about how to proceed in a discussion sequence are also the products of the interplay between teacher and students.

At Kleindorf High School (rural/small town), on the second day of discussion about the Teaching about White Privilege case, a student attempted to undermine the process from the beginning of class by challenging the significance of the issue.

MS. BREZEL: Is there a place in a high school classroom for something that is as controversial as the idea of white privilege?

WESTON: What is it?

MS. BREZEL: What is . . . ?

WESTON: [interrupting the teacher] I'm so lost about what they told us to do.

MS. BREZEL: OK. What is under this white privilege? Why are we so privileged to . . . ?

WESTON: Yeah. Why are you all up in arms about the whole topic? Nobody knows.

ALICIA: Can I explain?

MS. BREZEL: Go for it. Thank you.

ALICIA: It looks like perks and advantages that white people are supposed to get or whatever just because they are white. So like if students end up being in the school office and thinking the flesh color Band-Aid is supposed to look like the natural color for them, that is part of being a white. Band-Aid as "natural" is a symptom [class laughing]. If I stay in a hotel, the complimentary shampoo works on your hair but it doesn't work on my hair. That is one part. They make it work for white people. I don't even know how I would think about that, but again . . .

In Ms. Brezel's class, Weston had been absent from the small group preparation and the simulated meeting. He did not appear eager to catch up with his classmates, but challenged the usefulness and significance of talking about the issue that had been the focus of conversation on the previous days. For a moment, Ms. Brezel was taken aback, but another student was eager to respond and cared enough to explain to the classmate who had expressed the challenge. At other times in the discussion, Weston attempted to undermine the conversation, but Ms. Brezel carried on and appealed to the students who were invested in the process of deliberation. Students matter here in two ways: They can compromise the dialogue and they can protect and expand it. As challenging as Weston might seem to an observer, Ms. Brezel did not have a classroom of Westons and could trust the inquiry and dialogic processes to make the exchanges in class largely purposeful and supportive. Although Weston's dismissal of the issue as a genuine problem ("why are you all up in arms about the whole topic?") was something of an affront to the teacher and the class, Ms. Brezel did not attempt to suppress his skepticism, perhaps because it served a function in the process of deliberation. His challenge invited classmates to think about why the concept of white privilege is important to consider, and Ms. Brezel could rely on one of Weston's classmates to reply. In other words, the dynamic of a discussion-based inquiry exposed the skepticism and invited participants to voice the logical basis for their positions.

The Teacher Factor

As we discuss at length in Chapters 4 and 5, the teacher matters a great deal. This is not to say that as far as facilitating and connecting discussions some teachers just "have it" and others don't. Our observations of teachers in action and our reflections about our own practice over the years have revealed to us that the work that teachers do to plan for discussions in the near term and the long term, the orchestration of activities in class, and the decision making in the moment represent a substantial complex of thought and actions. While we discuss these details later in this book, we will show briefly here how teachers foster dialogue in two ways: (1) by protecting the supportive atmosphere of the classroom to encourage participation and to sponsor risk-taking, and (2) by consistently prompting dialogue by introducing problems, seeking contributions, and insisting on the development of thought.

As one example, we can look at the reaction of Ms. Widerhaken when one of her students becomes quite emotional about her reflection. When the discussion began to move away from the issue of teaching the concept of white privilege, Silvia reflected on her image as a hardworking student and inclusive classmate and how this image gives her a sense of pride but also makes her the target of ridicule.

SILVIA: When we were doing this social worker stuff [role playing], I say I am guilty of . . . [inaudible]. I don't feel like they are looking at me like "oh, yeah! That is when they talk about how your race is so bad and my race is great." I don't feel like you haven't thought about this. You don't feel like [inaudible] they don't look at her like she is trying to steal. And then they made him like, you know, I am just here. I don't feel like you cannot build a relationship across race. For everyone who looks at white people, they are bad also. I don't feel like every white person is horrible just like I don't think every black person is poor. I still feel like that it should be taught. You are going to think how you want about these things. Some people look at white people like they are all bad. I feel bad right now in this class saying that "white people, white people, white people." You don't know how you would feel towards whites. [suppressing tears]

MS. WIDERHAKEN: I am watching everybody's faces. I don't think there is a single white person sitting in this classroom right now that believes that you're labeling us, stereotyping us against the expected, you know, assuming things. OK? This is exactly why. You guys. The only thing that I am going to say is this: the thing that we bring up into the classroom, we bring this up because there are things that need to change. And it hurts my heart to hear you say that you think that is not going to change because everything that I do every day is based on the premise that it can change and it will, if we make it happen. And I truly believe you are the ones who can make that change.

In this potentially awkward moment, Ms. Widerhaken does not quickly change the focus to divert attention from Silvia. Instead, she affirms the feelings that Silvia harbors and speaks to her broader concern that others in the class believe that they can identify inequities and injustice and have the power to influence change. At this moment and as Ms. Widerhaken reported in a subsequent interview, she attempts to cultivate a sense of family in her classroom and sees this sense of community as essential to open inquiry.

At another level, teachers respond in ways that will extend thinking and support the integrity of an inquiry process. In the following exchange from Mr. Damon's class at suburban Mountbank High School, Mr. Damon presses students to support their claims and clarify their positions.

ANDREA: The reason was to help students learn how to interact with people from different cultures and different environments. So, my source is from the *Huffington Post*. So I had a quote from the source that says doing this [studying white privilege] in high school aims to help students understand themselves and their feelings and the beliefs of other individuals and groups. So, if they learn the feelings and beliefs of other people, it will be easier for them to get along with other people.

MR. DAMON: OK, that sounds like just what the article is saying. Can you explain your thinking?

ANDREA: Like, if you know how they are feeling, you're going to think about that before you interact. Like, from the source material, then they'll feel like the black kid. Like, why should there be white people [represented in ads and dolls], but not us?

MR. DAMON: Not 100 percent sure . . .

ANDREA: I don't know how else to explain it.

MR. DAMON: OK, so, I'm just a little bit confused about what you are saying. Can anyone else help Andrea out?

ANDREA: So, like, basically, what I'm saying is like, if you're going into feelings, if you like know how they're feeling, then other cultures other than you, like whites and other cultures and colors, how they interact, then you'll know how to interact with them.

MR. DAMON: OK, great, let's continue. Marilyn, did you get it?

MARILYN: I think what she means is that, white people are trying to get in the position of other cultures so that they know how other cultures are feeling.

MR. DAMON: So, it helps white people become more sympathetic. I wonder if it works the other way, too? Marilyn, you have a funny look on your face like that's an odd thing to say. Is that an odd thing to say?

MARILYN: Yeah.

MR. DAMON: White people don't need sympathy?

MARILYN: No, we're not saying that! It's just that in my view, white people don't get discriminated as much as other people do. So, like, it's kind of weird to think of us on the side of the white . . . I don't know!

In these exchanges with Andrea and Marilyn, Mr. Damon probes in a conversational way to encourage students to refine and clarify their positions. In some ways, Mr. Damon confesses that he doesn't understand and is looking for help. His questions do not signal that the students are wrong in their responses nor that they need to express his preferred position. His practice depends largely on paraphrasing to check for understanding, to ask questions to prompt elaboration, and to call on other students to support or evaluate the analysis of a peer.

If the discussion is indeed *authentic*, then the exchanges can take unexpected twists and turns. The sequence of exchanges is not scripted, so the teacher must think on his feet to decide at the moment to paraphrase, ask a variety of possible questions, offer an exception to a rule, summarize the ongoing discussion, or

Four Factors Affecting Discussion

Four obvious factors affect the extensiveness and quality of classroom discourse:

Students

Although the potential for extensive participation in authentic discussion does not depend on having a particularly academic and cooperative group of students, a teacher needs to pay attention to who the students are—the critical issues in their lives and in the lives of others in their community. It is hard to engage students in substantive discussions unless the issues seem consequential to the learners. The teacher also needs to be aware of each learner's particular strengths in order to organize functional groups and capitalize on students' knowledge and proficiencies.

Topic

We were able to survey high school students to discover what interests them. Teachers rely on a variety of means to learn what will prompt students' commitment to inquiry and discussion. We have recognized over decades of teaching that problems that feature issues about *justice, fairness, freedom, privacy, equity, identity,* and *obligation to authority* often resonate with adolescents. But we have also been surprised when the problem that seemed so compelling to us was passé to learners. We have learned to inquire and to honor students' interests as much as possible.

Structure

A consistent element in the lessons we observed across classes in four different schools was the same set of lesson plans for each teacher. The plans did not represent a "best practice" script, and the teachers varied the execution of the plans a bit, as was necessary in their particular context. But the teachers were consistent with the key elements: use a narrative to introduce a complex but "everyday" problem, structure a time in small groups for learners to examine data and prepare for discussion, facilitate a forum that featured competing points of view, and build on preceding discussions to synthesize arguments and arrive at considered judgments. The structure of the sequence ensured that the discussions built on each other: the small group preparation led to the simulated meeting; the simulated meeting exposed several views; a "debriefing" allowed for evaluation of the possibilities.

Teacher

The teacher's approach and moment-to-moment decisions are critical. During our time as supervisors in schools, we have witnessed classes in which the teacher turned a potentially dynamic discussion into a recitation or pathfinder journey toward the teacher's predetermined conclusions. As Nystrand suggests, a teacher makes a "dialogic bid" in inviting students into an authentic discussion. The dialogue continues as the teacher invites participants, asks follow-up questions, and honors established protocols. We say much more about the role of the teacher in Chapter 5.

call on another student. In student-managed discussions, the moves might look a bit different, but in this case, Mr. Damon was prompting students to follow certain protocols, such as providing evidence and elaboration and practicing uptake. We will discuss the details about these plans and practices in Chapter 5.

The teacher is an important factor, then—not in the sense of being a "gifted" facilitator but in the sense of being a prepared and reflective practitioner who envisions a long-term inquiry supported by daily dialogic discourse. The teacher as facilitator of sustained authentic discussion will have to have at hand a number of tools that she can draw on to support the dialogue.

The Activity Structure Factor

If we include Ms. Torino, all five teachers we observed followed a similar discussion sequence as part of a gateway experience into an inquiry-based unit of study. We know teachers who can enter class and initiate lively discussions by posing a provocative question or by noting some difficulty in interpreting a poem or a visual. As Juzwik, Borsheim-Black, Caughlan, and Heintz (2013) report, teachers rely on a variety of structures to encourage authentic discussions, even when difficulties challenge constructive deliberation. In implementing the instruction our university preservice students had developed, the teachers we observed followed a layered sequence that allowed for stages of exploring, drafting, applying, and refining. The orchestrated stages supported students in being prepared for each exchange. We judge that the structure of the inquiry activity itself accounts in part for the extent of participation and the elaboration in the contributions. In Chapters 4 and 5 we discuss in detail how teachers plan such discussion-based activities and how they manage the discussions.

A good deal of planning went into the discussions about the Robot Teacher and about the controversy over Teaching about White Privilege, but we can simplify for now by noting the three general stages: (1) The teacher relied on the case narrative to frame a problem and project how the initial discussions would serve as a gateway to subsequent readings, discussions, and writing. Then the teacher assigned students to specific viewpoints to prepare arguments as they imagined the characters would argue. In making these assignments, the teacher assured the students that their assigned role was temporary and that they would have an opportunity to express their personal views. The available data sets and the related readings supported this work in small groups. This preparation might require some work outside of class, including some communication among peers. (2) Having drafted their arguments in small groups, the students engaged in a simulated meeting (community stakeholders or district advisory meeting). The small group preparation makes this discussion substantial and displays the competing points of view regarding the focus question. (3) The third stage allows students to come out of character to evaluate the various arguments they have heard, combine some views where appropriate, and construct their own arguments in support of a particular policy.

The tight linkage across the discussions is important to consider. We can think of the scaffolding in this way: the third discussion as an extensive deliberation would not be possible without the simulated meeting to showcase the multiple viewpoints; the discussion in the simulated meeting would not be possible without the exploratory discussion in the small group preparation. Also, the small group preparation, because it involved only a few students in each group, encouraged the engagement and participation of all students from the start through a format that was less potentially intimidating than speaking to a whole class of students. In other words, one discussion built upon, and depended upon, the previous one. Again, the layering of discussions is not what we have commonly observed in schools. In addition, the prompt for students' written response to the problem emphasized the same procedures and language that students followed during the discussions that preceded the writing. We say more about this in Chapter 6.

The Subject Factor

The topic at the center of the discussion matters, but doesn't matter in a way that might seem obvious. In the case of Ms. Torino, and with the other four teachers we observed, the students in their classes voted by way of a survey to choose the focus for their inquiry. In each situation, we selected the top vote-getter and preservice teachers at the university developed the case and specified the structures for engaging in deliberation. We felt confident that the controversy about teaching the concept of white privilege would prompt lively discussions, and we judged that the topic was significant for adolescents in a diverse society to think thoroughly about. Mr. Damon reported that when his class completed the survey, an impromptu discussion erupted: "And that 'white privilege' scenario really seemed to strike a nerve!"

We have to inject a caution here. Consider the popular topics from the two survey opportunities. One sample of students chose to discuss the prospect of a school district investing in robot teachers; with the other sample, students chose to discuss the idea of teaching the concept of white privilege. These are distinct kinds of problems. While the Robot Teacher case might be intriguing to students, it was far less political and not as emotionally charged. We also have to keep in mind that among the eight choices in the second survey, only one was significantly less popular than all of the others. This tells us that most likely any one of seven choices could have sparked extended and connected conversations. In fact, by following a similar three-stage format, the teachers in our sample probably could have introduced any of the eight choices and engaged with students in substantial discussions that opened a line of inquiry across a unit of study. We have learned that the focus for discussions does not have to be a hot button issue, but it should honor students' interests. At the same time, teachers should not shy away from controversial subjects.

We caution that there is not necessarily a single high-priority subject that students need to discuss, even if we judge the topic to be one of grave consequence. The advice from our sample of teachers and the survey responses from two samples of students suggest to us some general considerations when choosing the focus for inquiry and discussion. First, teachers should be mindful of who their students are and judge what topics are likely to resonate with them. Learning about the learners may involve something as formal as a survey or may simply be the product of conversations with students and of discovery of who they are through their writing. We also suggest that there are perennial issues that tend to capture students' interest—e.g., friendship and other human relationships; the complications in forming identity; the need for freedom and privacy; the need for safety and security; the striving for fairness, equity, and justice; and the balance between the need to respect authority and advocating for one's own rights. In addition, the cases in this study all involve complex dilemmas with many nuances and potential complications, so there are numerous issues to unpack and no simple, clear-cut answers. The "perennial issues" that are likely to engage adolescents are all themes or issues explored in the literature that students encounter in schools and select on their own, and they are problems that are especially poignant when they occur in a school or local community context. For example, the Robot Teacher case ultimately concerned an issue about human relationships; and although the problem occurred in another school district, students inferred that the local high school might face the same situation in the future. While the white privilege controversy impacted a distant high school, the question applied in the sample of high schools where students discussed the case. One student at Kleindorf High School expressed surprise that teachers were already teaching the concept at his own high school; and a student at Stonebridge High School noted ruefully: "I am just feeling like we haven't been teaching it but we have already known, like when in 2016, I don't know, it is like it is starting to hurt me."

Summary

The one constant across the four classes was that they all discussed the appropriateness of teaching the concept of white privilege in a high school social studies class. The students read the same case narrative, had access to the same data sets, and consulted the same articles related to the case. The students followed a similar, if not identical, sequence of preparation and engagement in the discussions. The discussions across the four classes at four different high schools were not identical. But the discussions were extensive and connected. Students did most of the talking in each school. They supported claims by citing data, and they interpreted data. They listened actively to their classmates. Although inconsistent, they practiced uptake by acknowledging previous speakers and evaluating and building on their contributions. Again, students in all four schools—rural, suburban, and urban—were able to engage rationally, civilly, and productively in authentic discussions.

We looked at four factors in this chapter—students, activity structure, subject, and teacher. If you are a teacher in a middle school or high school, you do not control which students will be enrolled in your classes. There are several things you can do. You can discover what issues resonate with adolescents, connect those issues to a body of literature, and plan a serious program of inquiry about consequential problems. As we demonstrate in Chapter 4, there is a very accessible process for constructing the kind of inquiry-based activities that invited the students in the observed classes into extended conversation. Significantly, teachers can greatly influence the type of discourse that will dominate their classrooms, fostering a supportive environment and following procedures for building and sustaining discussions. Finally, teachers can extend students' inquiry and discussion with further reading and writing. The following chapters show how teachers accomplish these feats.

4

The Processes of Planning for Discussion: A Close Look at Teachers, Learners, and Activities

Surveys of students' interests guided the selection of the problems that provided the basis for the Robot Teacher and Teaching about White Privilege cases that we discuss in earlier chapters. As Deborah Stern (1995) suggests, this deference to students' interests requires a nimble teacher with the capacity to turn a general topic (e.g., a pugnacious mascot, robot teachers, white privilege) into a problem that students can appreciate in its full complexity and then use the initial discussions as the point of entry into a series of related texts and connected discussions. For example, if students chose to look into the prospect and wisdom of "making" someone fall in love with you (one of the survey choices), how does the teacher frame the topic as a problem that grabs learners, and how can that problem serve as the catalyst for weeks of connected conversations, related readings, and responsive writing? In this chapter, we follow the thinking of a teacher as she designs a problem-based activity that will stimulate much discussion that leads to elaborated writing. For us, as English educators, it is important that we are able to explain and model the practices of the teachers we have observed, so the remarks below will be rather prescriptive, although we intend them as general guidelines, knowing that different teachers follow different processes to construct learning activities. Table 4.1 outlines the steps that we and other teachers have followed to construct problem-based cases.

Often stories in the news, especially those that connect thematically to significant works of literature, have caught our attention. We worked with one teacher, Ms. Broussard, who was preparing for a summer English class that was intended to prepare incoming ninth graders for the routines and standards for academic work at the high school. Ms. Broussard knew that her class would include boys and girls who came from several different middle schools that sent students to the one big high school. With some experience with such ninth graders, Ms. Broussard knew that a perennial issue was for the students to leave their elementary school and middle school past and identity behind to start anew at the high school. Ninth grade was the time to make new impressions on new teachers, to form new friendships, and to construct a new, high school self. So, a

Table 4.1. Planning for Sustained Discussion

Step	Resource	Outcome
Survey students' interest	Constructed survey or informal scan	Established focus for inquiry and discussion
Construct case narrative	News stories, literature, films	Narrative that frames an inquiry problem
Describe roles/competing viewpoints	News stories and models of role-playing activities	Role descriptions
Identify and link related articles, videos, and/or other texts	Newspapers, newsmagazines, online publications, and videos	Links to related reading/viewing
Design forums and standards	Models of protocols for deliberations and collaborations	Discussion directions and rubric
Construct writing prompt	Models for written analyses of policy questions	Directions and rubric for written responses
Identify key academic vocabulary and potentially unfamiliar technical language	Case narrative, discussion directions, and writing prompt	List of key vocabulary, especially the words that prompt students' actions
Identify related texts that extend and complicate the inquiry	Novels, plays, short stories, poems, songs, films, television shows, photos, paintings, etc.	Constructed sequence of inquiry, reading, viewing, and discussion

predictable focus would be *identity*, a theme commonly represented in the literature that students read in high school. But how could Ms. Broussard represent this broad topic in a way that provoked learners to discuss extensively, read broadly and carefully, and write elaborately?

Constructing the Narrative

We know that teachers find a variety of means for prompting discussions—e.g., list of questions, journal reflections, provocative passages from literature, a scene from a film, a case study. In the examples that we report in this book, teachers have relied on cases that prompted discussions and relied on a role-playing forum as part of the sequence. This is only one possibility, but we have found that the role-playing structures in the classes we observed allowed for inclusive perspectives and the kind of challenges that invite participants to support their claims and evaluate the arguments of others. In the example we offer here, the related news stories that caught Ms. Broussard's attention reported the practice of "predictive policing" used in major cities across the United States. We wanted the stories to be available to students to inform their understanding and refine their judgment about the practices, but we feared that any one news article could suggest that problems have been resolved or that one perspective on the problem should have authority above others. In other words, using a single perspective on the problem could make the situation less problematic and less debatable.

We also wanted the problem to seem immediate and critical for the learners. Our typical response to this challenge is to write a narrative that sets the problem in a school where the actions of others can have a negative or beneficial impact on students like the ones in our classes or in Ms. Broussard's class. Ms. Broussard recognized that the practice of predictive policing—the use of a substantial body of data and analytics to anticipate crimes and to identify and monitor specific residents who might be inclined to commit crimes in the future—might seem a bit removed from the lives of students who don't typically concern themselves with the policies practiced by big police departments. But the idea of using data to predict future behavior has long been the practice in schools. SAT and ACT exams are predicated on the idea that the current data predict future behavior. Similarly, schools use various placement test results and grades to place students in specific classes—in some cases channeling students toward a future of manual labor and minimum wages or down a path toward a college degree and higher earnings. In fact, it has long surprised us that administrators have not used the data more proactively and constructively to match students with the teachers, resources, supports, and instruction that they need to have a more positive and successful experience in high school. In working collaboratively with Ms. Broussard on the activity, we realized that if we focused on disciplinary matters alone and took the predictive practices to an extreme, we could offer students a narrative that hits close to home and gets their attention. We provide the resulting "Predictive Discipline" narrative here and then discuss the features that we have built in, features that would likely be in any case narrative that prompts discussion and debate.

Predictive Discipline: Can a Principal Stop Problems Before They Happen?

In schools, can adults know which students are going to cause problems and stop the problems before they occur? Dr. Julius Sterling, principal of Floodrock High School, thinks so. Stories about "predictive policing" in Memphis, Santa Cruz, and Chicago have intrigued Dr. Sterling. The idea of "predictive analysis" behind predictive policing is that the statistical trends related to people, places, and situations can allow one to predict when and where a crime is likely to occur and who is likely to be involved in the crime. In other words, *police can predict a crime before it happens.* For example, in Santa Cruz, California, a staff statistician was able to alert patrol officers when and where someone was likely to break into cars at a downtown parking garage. Acting on the prediction, police officers drove to the site and apprehended two suspects who were attempting to enter a car—one suspect with an outstanding arrest warrant and another in possession of a sizeable quantity of drugs. In Chicago, predictive analysis allowed police officers in a wide sweep to arrest 140 individuals suspected of involvement with gun violence crimes; their past behavior suggested that these residents were likely to be in illegal possession of firearms.

Principal Sterling, a former math teacher, recognized that he could follow similar practices in order to make Floodrock High School safer and more orderly. He has access to a large body of information on each student, going back to the time when each one was in kindergarten. He knows, for example, that students who were often tardy and absent during the primary grades of elementary school will continue to be tardy and absent often in high school. But that was just the start. Dr. Sterling's analysis allowed him to identify areas of the school and surrounding community where infractions and crimes were most likely to occur and when they would occur. Dr. Sterling could predict which students were likely to bully others or who would likely be victims of bullying. He could tell you which students were likely to engage in fights with others and which students were probably going to be openly disrespectful toward teachers in classrooms. He also had strong suspicions about which students were likely to use drugs or alcohol and which students were likely to steal from fellow students or from adults working in the school.

Dr. Sterling's predictions are based on *correlations*: that is, when one factor is present, another is likely to follow. In an informal way, poker players use this analysis, perhaps noticing that when another player has a good hand, she always scratches her nose. College entrance exams work this way, with studies from many previous years suggesting the scores associated with success in the first year of college: reaching a certain threshold score suggests that you will do well at the start of college. Dr. Sterling has been experimenting informally with the "predictive discipline" by contacting parents of students who are likely to be absent or tardy often and by increasing the adult presence at certain times in areas where students are likely to cause trouble (e.g., fighting or exchanging drugs).

Realize that Dr. Julius Sterling is an influential figure in the state. Other principals look to his example to imitate in their own school. If he enacts his "predictive discipline" plan and can show a positive effect in deterring infractions before they happen, there is a *good chance that the principal in your school will soon follow his example.* If the community accepts Dr. Sterling's plan, it might signal the direction of all schools in the future.

Expanded Practice: Encouraged by his informal study of "predictive discipline," Dr. Sterling has decided to expand the practice in these ways:

- **PHONE CALLS:**
  - Identify the students who are likely to be frequently absent and/or tardy and place repeated automatic phone calls to their homes to wake them up in the morning and urge them to get to school on time.
- **SPECIALIZED "LOCKDOWNS":**
  - Identify students who are *likely* to use drugs or alcohol and prevent them from leaving the school during the school day, even if they are seniors.
  - Identify students who are *likely* to use drugs or alcohol and prevent them from receiving hall passes for bathroom use.
  - Identify students who are *likely* to vandalize the school and prevent them from receiving hall passes for bathroom use.
  - Identify students who are *likely* to bully others or be violent, and prohibit them from field trips where their supervision would be less attentive than it would be at school.
- **SEARCHING AND SEIZING PERSONAL BELONGINGS:**
  - Identify students who are *likely* to bring drugs to school and use trained dogs to search their lockers for drugs.

- Identify students who are *likely* to steal and search their lockers frequently while they are in class.
- Identify students who are *likely* to bring weapons to school and search their lockers at random times.

- **INCREASED MONITORING OF "PROBLEM" STUDENTS:**
  - Before the school year begins, give teachers a list of those students who are *likely* to be disrespectful, and establish a rapid response system for paraprofessional security to go to the classroom to remove the student.
  - Before the school year begins, identify students who are *likely* to bully other students and assign them to designated seating in the cafeteria so that they can be closely monitored.
  - Before the school year begins, identify students who are *likely* to be the victims of bullying and assign them a peer mentor to help them move safely through the school.

Potential Controversy: Dr. Sterling knows that there is likely to be some confusion about the idea of "predictive discipline," and he anticipates that there will be some opposition. Being of a democratic temperament, Dr. Sterling has called together some important stakeholders to discuss his proposed plan. He has composed a committee of people who have various interests and opinions about the proposed plan. Dr. Sterling believes that their deliberations will inform him and the community about the viability of "predictive discipline."

Data Sets

Recognizing that responsible critical thinkers base their judgments on information and analysis, Ms. Broussard provided learners with information about the high school, common discipline problems in school, and the practices and concerns about the comparable predictive policing practices. We present the information as tables, charts, bullet lists, and links to online articles. A look at online school reports and simple Google searches will provide information about typical high schools and list articles about predictive policing. Making sure students read the information is an important part of the preparation for discussion. The summary information about the school appears in concise format, and the related news stories will take the form of narratives. The news articles can become quickly dated, so any teacher who chooses to use the Predictive Discipline case will want to search for more current articles related to the problem. In Ms. Broussard's case, after she formed collaborative teams, she directed each team to read a specific article to support their arguments. Here are the data sets for the Predictive Discipline case:

Related Information: The following information should help you in thinking about the case and preparing for discussion. The information appears in Figure 4.1 and Table 4.2 in three forms: (1) demographic information about the school, (2) disciplinary trends in high schools, and (3) related news stories and reports available online.

Figure 4.1. Floodrock High School demographics. (Source: Interactive Illinois Report Card)

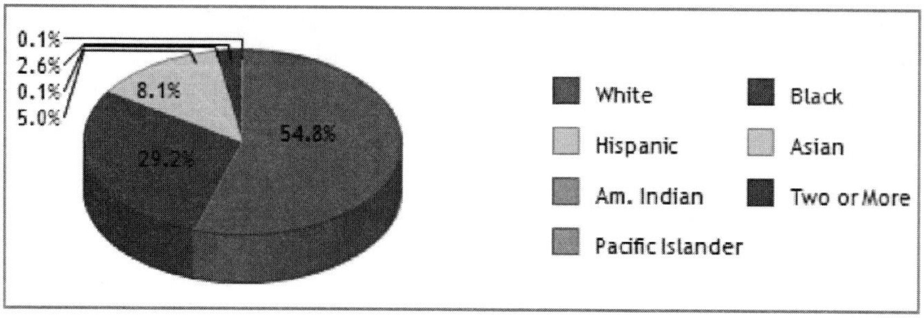

Table 4.2. School Demographic Summary (Source: Interactive Illinois Report Card)

Enrollment	1,582
Percent Low Income	54.5%
White	54.8%
Black	29.2%
Hispanic	8.0%
Asian	2.6%
American Indian	0.1%
Pacific Islander	0.1%
Two or More	<1%

Common Discipline Problems in High School:

- Theft, especially from lockers
- Fighting/threatening violence
- Bullying and hazing
- Cheating; plagiarism
- Drug use
- Alcohol use
- Parking and other driving-related violations
- Disrespect toward adult staff
- Misuse of technology
- Vandalism
- Chronic absences
- Chronic tardiness

Related Sources and Discussions:

"Can Predictive Policing Be Ethical and Effective?" *New York Times*, November 18, 2015. (Also see related commentary.)

Davey, Monica, & Mitch Smith. "140 Are Arrested in Gang Raids in Chicago." *New York Times*, May 20, 2016.

Eligon, John, & Timothy Williams. "Police Program Aims to Pinpoint Those Most Likely to Commit Crimes." *New York Times*, September 24, 2015.

Goode, Erica. "Sending the Police Before There's a Crime." *New York Times*, August 15, 2011.

Lartey, Jamiles. "Predictive Policing Practices Labeled as 'Flawed' by Civil Rights Coalition." *The Guardian*, August 31, 2016.

"Predictive Policing: Don't Even Think about It." *The Economist*, July 20, 2013.

Saunders, Jessica. "Pitfalls of Predictive Policing." RAND Corporation, October 11, 2016.

Features of the Case Narrative

In collaboration with Ms. Broussard, the ninth-grade teacher, we composed this school-based problem. While we could not make the claim that the predictive discipline practice was occurring in the students' own school, we noted that the practices at another high school, where there is an influential principal, could set an example that the administrators in their own school could soon follow. We described the basis for the practice and offered details about how predictive discipline practices could impact students. By the end of the narrative, we noted that some critics would oppose Dr. Sterling and briefly offered the basis for that opposition. So the narrative has these basic elements: the *story* that includes a specific *setting*; principal *players*; central *actions*; a *conflict*; *details* about the actions, setting, and conflict (i.e., data sets); and the basis for *opposition*. We judge that, unlike a question alone, a narrative allows learners to see the intended benefits from a policy and the potential harms to individuals. The case also provides sufficient information to help students reflect on the potential harms and weigh the potential benefits against the likely harms. We judge that the narrative helps students to contend with a series of questions. The case, then, offers these prompts for preparation and discussion:

The central question now is this: *Should Dr. Sterling initiate an aggressive plan for "predictive discipline"?* This central question connects with other related questions:

- To what extent will Dr. Sterling's plan likely make the school a safer and more orderly place for everyone?
- How is it possible that anyone can be unjustly harmed by the execution of the plan?
- How reliable is it that someone can depend on past behavior as a predictor of future behavior?
- To what extent will Dr. Sterling's plan actually work? Is it a *workable* plan? What problems or complications do you anticipate?
- If you can anticipate that Dr. Sterling's plan will cause more harm than good, who is likely to be harmed and how significant will that harm be?

You probably already have some tentative answers to these questions; but for a scheduled meeting, you will need to inform your opinions with some information. You will want to offer evidence for any claims that you make, and you will want to anticipate what others will say to argue against your position.

Directing Collaboration and Discussion

As we discuss in detail in Chapter 3, a teacher needs to plan for a connected sequence of discussion, with each stage of discussion preparing students for the next. Ms. Broussard projected the discussions to follow in three stages: (1) small group preparation to argue from an assigned point of view; (2) a simulated meeting to showcase the competing perspectives on the problem; and (3) a debriefing in which students argue from their own points of view, taking into account the perspectives they heard in the previous discussion.

Experience tells us not to put students into hastily organized groups and direct them to discuss a question. We wanted students to know the overall plan and sequence, and we wanted them to know specifically what they would be expected to do at each stage in the process. We offer this caution and reassurance about assigning roles and engaging in role-play: While students might be hesitant to assume a perspective they do not personally embrace, they are more willing to play the role briefly when they know that they will ultimately have an opportunity to argue about the case and central issues from their own perspectives. Our experience has been that most students can appreciate the idea that exposure to an array of competing views will ultimately strengthen any position they maintain. We know, and are encouraged, that students frequently shift and refine their personal positions as they hear arguments from several perspectives.

We offer here the sets of directions for discussion. The directions are a start, and any teacher will rely on her own means for managing students' collaborations and deliberations. We advise that the questions that direct discussions should align with the expectations for a written response and with a model for reasoning. In other words, if you expect that in their writing, students in the long run will support a proposition, interpret the evidence offered as support, represent opposing views accurately, and evaluate those views fairly, then the questions that prompt and advance discussion should ask students to make these moves in their spoken responses. The questions should encourage the procedures (i.e., summarize, support, interpret, evaluate) that transfer to a written analysis of the case. As Ms. Broussard entered into discussions with her ninth graders, she wanted to see that students could summarize the problem, note the possible harms (from not enacting Dr. Sterling's plans or from enacting it), measure the significance or impact of those harms, weigh the likely benefits against the potential harms, represent fairly and honestly the opposing views, and assess those views. The directions should prompt the students' discussion to reveal whether the students are thinking rationally, interacting civilly, and proceeding inclusively. In short, the questions for discussion should align with learning outcomes and with the teacher's assessment efforts.

Directions for discussing the case in three ways: As with many difficult situations we may find ourselves in, it is useful to start by imagining the thinking from the several perspectives in the case. The class will discuss the central question in *three phases*:

Stage 1: *Small group preparation:* In order for you to contribute to discussion with the whole class, you will need to form a decision and construct a logical argument to support it. With two or three other members of your class, prepare an argument from the point of view of a single character. Your argument should attend to the following questions:

1. What harms is Dr. Sterling trying to correct? Are these problems significant? How do you know? (Rely on the available information to support your claims.)

2. Is Dr. Sterling's plan likely to accomplish the goal of making the school a safer and more orderly place? How do you know? (Draw on your reading to support your prediction.)
3. Is Dr. Sterling's plan likely to work? Where do you see problems, if any, in its execution? (Draw from your reading and project what is likely to happen.)
4. What alternatives, if any, can you offer to replace what Dr. Sterling has in mind? If you agree with the goal to make the school a safer place, what can you offer that would be better than Dr. Sterling's plan?
5. What arguments do you anticipate the other meeting attendees will make? How will you respond to these arguments?

Reminder: Be sure to take notes as you prepare so that you are ready with a coherent argument when the entire class discusses the case.

Stage 2: *Committee Forum:* Enter into a discussion with the whole class to listen to the arguments of others and to advance your own position. If everyone is to arrive at a deeper understanding through negotiation, it is important that everyone has a chance to speak without interruption. It is also critical that you are able to *connect* your contribution by *citing the position of someone else* with whom you either agree or disagree to some extent.

1. The superintendent will call the meeting to order and explain the format for the hearing.
2. Speakers will follow the superintendent's procedure for sharing at the meeting. They will offer their positions on the issue of predictive policing or predictive discipline, support their positions with evidence and reasoning, and connect their ideas to other speakers' by thoughtfully "uptaking" (i.e., referring to others) them with connections or questions.
3. After all attendees have had significant time both to offer their own views and listen to the views of others, the meeting will conclude.
4. Since the superintendent is concerned that everyone in the room understands each other, he makes it a point to ask many thoughtful follow-up questions of each speaker. The superintendent likes board meetings and committee meetings to be orderly, fair, and respectful; he will make sure each participant has an equal opportunity to talk, and he will ask for quiet from any speakers out of order.

Reminders: Be faithful to the role you have been assigned, but also, be yourself. When you are listening, take careful notes about the main idea each character offers. Take time, while listening, to think about the case from your OWN point of view: Should Dr. Sterling execute his plan? Why or why not?

Stage 3: *Be yourself:* Although you have imagined the case from an assigned point of view, you might not agree with this point of view, or you may have changed your thinking after you have had a chance to hear other thinkers. In this stage of discussion, you will abandon your assigned role and think about the case from your own point of view: Should Dr. Sterling expand the practice of predictive discipline as specified in his plan? What evidence do you have that the plan is likely to work or not work? Does a person's past behavior accurately predict future behavior? Is it possible for a person to change his or her behavior significantly over time? If we identify someone as a troublemaker, will that person and others continue to think of that person as a troublemaker for the rest of the student's life? To what extent is Dr. Sterling's plan likely to accrue some benefits for the students and staff at the school? To what extent is the plan likely to cause more harm than good? Are there any viable alternatives to the plan that Dr. Sterling has outlined? In the end, what action do you recommend?

Characters and Points of View

In our long teaching careers, we have discussed many problem cases, with or without accompanying role-playing, and, as discussed in Chapter 3, we have discovered distinct value in the role-playing. As students have reported to us, the role-playing places learners in a position to imagine how others are affected by the policy and how they are reacting to the problem. The dynamic interplay of the simulated meeting allows the students to showcase the various and competing perspectives. Students commonly report that this deliberation exposes them to arguments that they would not have thought about independently. The meeting often influences students to shift their positions, and the exposure to several arguments almost always helps students to refine their thinking.

In working with Ms. Broussard, we suggested several points of view, offered in the most general form: e.g., the parent of a student who has often been suspended, an honors student, a dean, a classroom teacher. Ms. Broussard suggested additional roles and provided details for the role descriptions. There are three important considerations here. First, there are essentially two sides of the question about the proposed policy—accept it or reject it—but there are more nuanced positions as to the bases for acceptance or rejection. We wanted to represent the complex of positions and make sure there was an even distribution on both sides of the question. Second, we wanted there to be enough detail to show students why the characters would assume the positions that they did, but we didn't want to lay out arguments in such detail that students would simply read from their role descriptions. In each case, the role description should serve as a prompt to allow a team of students to construct their own arguments, based on a set of guiding questions (see Stage 2 above). Third, we have tried *not* to assign students with a role that they find repugnant. This consideration was especially important in the Teaching about White Privilege case. For example, we did not want to place any students in the role of arguing a viewpoint such as white privilege is an earned and deserved privilege because of the superiority of whites to all others. In the Predictive Discipline case, students may disagree with an assigned position, but it seems unlikely that they would find that assuming any of the characters would compromise their moral, ethical, or political sensibilities. With more volatile issues, the potential offense and resistance are more probable and a teacher would have to adjust the role description or carefully choose to whom she assigns a role. The following descriptions suggest that the character is either male or female, but the participants can obviously assume the gender identity as they wish to represent the character: e.g., the mom could be a dad, the NHS president could be a boy or a girl. Here, then, are the perspectives that we offered about the Predictive Discipline case:

Board Meeting Attendees

1. *School Superintendent:* The superintendent of the Floodrock School District ultimately supervises the teachers and principals in the district, but the members of the Floodrock School Board have selected her for this position. Before the meeting, she will have thoroughly researched articles and reports related to predictive policing to make sure she understands the implications of the situation. To maintain an unbiased stance, the superintendent will not offer an argument at the hearing, but instead, will manage the speakers, being certain that both sides have had a chance to share their points of view. She wants to be careful both to support Dr. Sterling, an important member of her administrative team, and to respect the possible opposition within the school and within the community.
2. *Principal:* Dr. Sterling will present his case to the community that Predictive Policing is the best way to ensure safety, security, and positive outcomes

for Floodrock students, staff, and the community at large. Dr. Sterling will be certain to support his position by referencing articles and reports that demonstrate the benefits of Predictive Policing; he will also cite statistics about infractions in high schools and call upon his fifteen years' experience as a principal to explain why he thinks Predictive Discipline is necessary in all high schools.

3. *P.E. Teacher:* As a ten-year veteran of Floodrock High School and an FHS grad himself, the P.E. teacher is in favor of the changes predictive policing will bring. He is still bothered by the Great Kickball Foul of 2014, in which the answers to his very difficult, end-of-term Kickball Skills Test were leaked to the whole school via Facebook. On more than one occasion, students have been found in possession of dangerous items, including drugs, in their gym lockers. FHS did not have problems of this scale when he attended the school. This teacher fears that if something is not done now, the next ten years will be even worse for him and his students.

4. *Librarian:* The librarian is gravely concerned about the implications of Predictive Policing. While he has certainly seen his share of issues in the library—contraband food, inappropriate technology use, horseplay, and the like—he also doesn't think that Predictive Policing is the answer. He has read too many books and has seen too many movies about the risks of monitoring people to believe that Mr. Sterling's proposal will make things better. In fact, he fears it will have unintended consequences and make things much worse, just as similar efforts have had in communities across America.

5. *National Honor Society (NHS) President:* The president of the National Honor Society has worked hard to earn her position in NHS and as president; threats of violence, bullying, theft, cheating, and other ills at FHS have not made her journey easy. As NHS president, she will not only represent her own voice but also the voices of many students, some of them NHS members as well, who have suffered by either facing unsafe or unfair situations, or by being afraid of unsafe and unfair situations.

6. *President, Student Congress:* The president of Student Congress views it as his job to represent the common student's voice. As such, he has heard many complaints from students throughout the school—from three-sport athletes to chess club members; strong students to struggling students; ninth graders to seniors—about the proposed Predictive Discipline policy and its effects on their privacy, safety, and reputations. He will argue

against Dr. Sterling's proposed changes, noting especially that a person can change and should not be labeled forever.

7. *Resident/ Camp Director:* This longtime resident has worked for the popular summer camp, Camp Tekalya, for twenty years, first as a counselor and now as the camp director. She also lives in the Floodrock community; her own children recently graduated from FHS. Many of her campers attend Camp Tekalya for several summers in a row, and she has seen with her own eyes how much children can change as they approach adulthood. This local resident has often worked with adolescents and is now concerned that Predictive Policing will introduce permanent, serious consequences for adolescents who need permission to make mistakes occasionally as they grow up.

8. *Community Member:* This community member owns a house adjacent to the FHS campus and has lived there for more than fifty years. Recent news reports of national increases in crime statistics and drug use have made him concerned about the safety of students and neighbors near the school. He also worries about the welfare of students and the adults in the school. This interested community member is in favor of any measures that will ensure security and peace.

9. *Parent:* This parent's son recently enrolled in Floodrock High School after transferring from a neighboring school, where he had suffered relentless bullying from a small group of students, bullying that did not end despite school consequences. Though the child is currently thriving at FHS, his mom is concerned about the risk of bullying in this environment, too—not just for the one child, but for any Floodrock student. She is in support of school policy that can prevent bullying before it begins.

Prompting a Written Response

In constructing the directions for discussion and in monitoring students' responses throughout the deliberation processes, we have kept in mind our expectations for a written response. A realistic consideration is that when we assess students' written responses, the learners would already be familiar with the criteria for that assessment. In a sense, as Wiggins and McTighe (2005) have posited, the assessment in itself represents a detailed expression of the goals that we set for learning, and we want those goals to be as clear as possible for learners.

We have offered two sets of prompts below. The first set prompts students to write an argument in response to a policy question—a question about what *action* to take in response to a current problem. Since we like to offer students options and we recognize that students' viable written responses do not always have to be arguments, we suggest several possibilities, including a narrative and a conversation.

Writing about the case: After you have discussed the case at length, you should be prepared to write to the appropriate audience to offer advice about the central question: *Should Dr. Sterling enact his plan for "predictive discipline"?*

You might want to write to Dr. Sterling, to the district superintendent, or to members of the School Board. In any case, your written response should have the following elements:

An introduction: Even if your reader is familiar with the case, you will want to provide a brief summary of the situation and the problem. The summary should allow someone who is not familiar with the case to understand the central conflict. You will also want to express a position about the central question in the case.

A review of possible actions: As your class discussion probably revealed, everyone does not agree about what should happen. Review the arguments you have heard about the central question in the case, even if you don't agree with them. Explain why people have taken the positions they have taken; but if you disagree, explain why you disagree with their reasoning.

An argument for your own position: Show your reader that after you have reviewed all possibilities, you have judged that, on balance, your recommendation is the best one. You should support any claims that you make, and explain any evidence that you offer by referring to established rules or principles. Your argument might show that your recommended course of action offers the greatest benefit and the fewest disadvantages.

A conclusion: To close your discussion, you will want to remind your readers about the issues involved in the case and reiterate your position.

Precision and propriety: The tone and appearance of your written response contribute to its persuasiveness. This means that the writing should be organized, logical, and coherent. This also means that mistakes in usage and punctuation should not cause confusion. Share a draft of your composition with another reader (e.g., classmate, family member, or friend) to check for precision and clarity. Invite the reader also to comment on the tone of the writing: Do you "sound" appropriately respectful for the audience you are addressing? Use the feedback from your reader to edit your work, and perhaps to revise it.

Alternative Written Responses: As an alternative or addition to the suggested written response outlined above, you might choose from the following options:

- As a regular blogger, you like to use your online forum to share with the world your opinions about curious stories in the news. For your blog, report the essential details of the case, evaluate the competing arguments, and argue for your recommended course of action.
- Imagine you are the president of the School Board rendering a decision about this case. You would be addressing all of the interested parties, revealing that you have taken all arguments into consideration. In the end, you will explain how you arrived at a decision.
- Imagine what would happen to one representative student who might fall victim to the "predictive discipline" policy. Tell the story of this person. What has happened to the character in the past to be identified as a potential victim or perpetrator? What has happened to the character recently, how has he/she reacted, and what are likely to be the long-term consequences? As with any good story, your narrative should provide sufficient detail to help the reader imagine the characters, situation, and actions. The narrative should include some realistic dialogue. Your story should be realistic enough to allow a reader to believe that the events could very well happen to someone. Readers are likely to appreciate a bit of suspense and will like that the sequence of events follows in a sensible order.
- Imagine a meeting between a teacher who supports the "predictive discipline" policy and the skeptical parent of one of the teacher's students. Represent the conversation as a movie or play script, with both the dialogue and the stage directions that reveal gestures, movement, and attitude. The conversation should highlight the arguments and feelings on both sides and suggest a likely outcome for the current drama.

A Word about Vocabulary

The various directions in the case prompt students' actions, which enable the teacher to observe and assess, whether the actions are the team collaboration, the role-playing, the deliberation, or the written response. If the prompted actions are the bases for assessment and represent learning goals, it is only fair to ensure that students know the language that prompts their actions. As part of the process of constructing the activity, we suggest that the teacher scan all of the written material (i.e., case narrative, discussion directions, role descriptions, data sets, and writing prompts) to anticipate the vocabulary that students are likely to be less familiar with. In this case, Ms. Broussard identified key vocabulary that falls under two categories—words in the directions and words in the case. The first category represents the abstract academic language that directs behavior. This is language that has specific use and meaning in a school setting. For this case, we judge that a teacher will want to make sure students are familiar with the following words and phrases: *argue, cite evidence, express a position, interpret evidence, summarize,* and *support claims.* Again, predicting students' familiarity with a set of vocabulary will depend on the teachers' knowledge of the learners. In this case, Ms. Broussard judged that her ninth graders might stumble with the following words: *accrue, analysis, correlation, demographics, deter, predictive, temperament,* and *threshold.*

The wisest advice we have received about teaching vocabulary in support of reading comes from Kylene Beers (2003). She notes as anomalous the practice of a teacher demanding that students learn vocabulary that the teacher never uses herself as part of the daily discourse of the classroom. We know that students have to be exposed to vocabulary in a variety of contexts before they internalize it. We suggest, then, that as the introduction to the case approaches, the teacher try to use in class words such as *correlation, demographics, deter,* and *predictive* so that students hear the words, recognize the context for their use, and understand the concepts that these words represent.

Literature, Film, and the Expanding Inquiry Unit

The teachers we have observed have used discussion-based activities like the role-playing and deliberations about the Predictive Discipline case both to prepare students for elaborated writing and as a means for building background knowledge that situated learners for critical thinking as they entered a unit of inquiry into related themes. The issues at the core of the Predictive Discipline case have probably reminded the reader about several related stories, novels, and films. In Ms. Broussard's case, she planned a sequence of readings and viewings that would move students from relatively simple understandings to more complex ruminations about identity, profiling, personal liberty, and the possible overreach of authority, and she invited students to identify stories and films that the case made them think about.

We have listed some possibilities below, in no particular order. We judge that an English teacher will be able to add to this list, generate other possibilities, and schedule the reading so that the introduction of each text complicates the inquiry by adding a new dimension or consideration. Here is our list of possibilities:

"The Minority Report" by Philip K. Dick, in *The Minority Report and Other Classic Stories*

Minority Report, a film by Steven Spielberg

The Adjustment Bureau, a film by George Nolfi

"Adjustment Team" by Philip K. Dick, in *Adjustment Team and Other Stories*

A Clockwork Orange by Anthony Burgess (and Stanley Kubrick's film interpretation)

1984 by George Orwell

The Giver by Lois Lowry

Brave New World by Aldous Huxley

Anthem by Ayn Rand

Harry Potter series by J. K. Rowling

Fahrenheit 451 by Ray Bradbury

Beyond Freedom and Dignity by B. F. Skinner

Review of the Process

If tomorrow morning you were to find a case in the news that links to a line of inquiry that is likely to resonate with your students, how would you build on the news story to design a carefully scaffolded sequence of discussions that serve as a gateway to writing and to a broader unit of inquiry? In this chapter we have shared the processes that we, in collaboration with a high school teacher, have followed in designing one discussion-based activity. These are the processes that we have followed on many occasions in constructing a variety of case studies and role-playing activities. We have identified some principles of design by reflecting on our own practice and by looking to models from Troyka (1974), Troyka and Nudelman (1975), McCann (2014), and McCann, D'Angelo, Galas, and Greska (2015). In summary, if you want to construct activities that are likely to prompt and sustain discussion and begin the path toward broader inquiry, here are some key elements:

- Identify a problem that resonates with adolescents, and convert this problem into a *narrative*, with characters, setting, and conflict.
- Provide learners with access to the *information* they need to think about the problem and support a position.
- Identify competing points of view to examine the problem and proposed policies through *multiple lenses*.
- Specify the *protocols* for discussing the problem, in a sequenced way that builds on itself.
- Provide for *assessment* practices that look for evidence of the kinds of *procedures* that are likely to transfer to writing, prepare learners for critical thinking, and immerse them in ongoing civil discourse.
- Provide students with directions and options for a *written response* to the problem.
- Connect the discussions to subsequent readings and viewings, as part of *sustained inquiry* into consequential questions.

We hope that this review, which requires both task analysis and activity analysis, provides help in constructing the tools necessary to initiate, sustain, connect, and assess extensive discussion. But having the activity in hand is just the beginning. In the next two chapters, we discuss how teachers can create the environment that encourages students to participate and how teachers can make wise, supportive decisions from moment to moment in keeping the conversation dialogic and moving it along to promote thorough thinking and deep understanding.

5 The Complex of Teacher Moves, across the Year and in the Moment

What do teachers do to generate the high levels of student engagement and interaction in authentic discussion that we have seen in the previous chapters? Designing instructional activities, such as inquiry-based sequences, that promote discussion is key. However, even though carefully designed activities that meet the criteria described in previous chapters are a necessary component, there are additional factors that are also important. Through observing the teachers in their classrooms, conducting interviews with them, and reflecting on our own decades of experience observing teachers and classrooms, we examine two broad areas that are involved in effectively prompting and promoting authentic discussion: (1) ways that teachers create a classroom environment in which students feel their contributions are valued and respected by everyone, and (2) moves that teachers make as discussions are unfolding to ignite, nurture, and sustain the dialogue.

Creating a Classroom Environment for Authentic Discussion

First, teachers who create a classroom environment conducive to and focused on authentic discussion have a clear and specific vision of what authentic discussion looks like and what they want to see occurring. What is their vision and what is their conception of what it means to engage in authentic classroom discussion?

We have talked with many English language arts teachers over our careers, and almost every English language arts teacher states that his or her primary mode of instruction, preferred mode of instruction, and/or best mode of instruction is "discussion." But digging deeper, we find that there are differences in what "discussion" means to different teachers. We are reminded of an observation and interview George Hillocks cites in which he observed a classroom with virtually nothing but teacher talk. He says the teacher informed him later in an interview the same day that the class had had "quite a good discussion" on this day. Hillocks reports that he had made notes of student contributions and had only one indication of a student talking: The student had come into class late and apologized for his tardiness. Hillocks explains: "No other comments from students at all, and yet the teacher regarded the class as a 'good discussion'" (qtd. in McCann, 2014, p. xi).

We have observed teachers carry on an extended conversation with one or a few students while the rest of the class is silent and refer to the class as having "a great discussion." And it is not uncommon for teachers to call a recitation a good or lively discussion. By recitation, we are referring to a pattern of classroom talk distinct from authentic discussion. It involves teachers initiating a question, most often a question asked for which the teacher has a specific answer or the contours of an answer in mind. A student is called on and gives a response, and the teacher evaluates the response ("that's right," "good," "yes," or "not exactly, does anyone else have an idea about this?" and so forth). This pattern has also been called IRE (for Initiate, Respond, Evaluate) or an oral quizzing of students rather than an authentic inquiry in which teacher and students explore genuine questions that don't have predetermined or pre-scripted answers (Nystrand, 1997, 2006; Applebee, Langer, Nystrand, & Gamoran, 2003; McCann, Johannessen, Kahn, & Flanagan, 2006; McCann, 2014). In recitation, student responses tend to be relatively short, often only a few words. Frequently, in evaluating student responses, teachers may elaborate on the student answers, including additional information that they were looking for, launching what amounts to a mini-lecture. In these cases, the proportion of teacher talk during the class is much greater than the proportion of student talk.

In differentiating authentic discussion from other types of classroom talk such as recitation or lecture, we are not making judgments about the value or appropriateness of these other activities within specific contexts; the point we want to make is that "discussion" as an instructional activity can mean very different things to different people. But we have found that the way teachers define and conceptualize discussion seems to make a difference in terms of what happens in classrooms.

The teachers we observed generally have a clear vision of what they consider a "good discussion." Though they didn't necessarily use the terms *authentic* or *dialogic discussion* versus *recitation* or *IRE*, their vision of a "good discussion" corresponds to the characteristics of authentic discussion (McCann, 2014; McCann, Johannessen, Kahn, & Flanagan, 2006; Nystrand, 2006; Applebee, Langer, Nystrand, & Gamoran, 2003). We present a list of these characteristics in Figure 5.1.

Figure 5.1. What makes an authentic discussion?

- Students are engaged in talking about an academic concept, problem, or issue.
- Teachers invite students to communicate their ideas and their thinking about a "problem" or "issue" without teachers having a set right or wrong answer in mind.
- Teachers are "invitational" in interacting with students and avoid being "inquisitional" or "interrogational" (Walsh, 2017).
- Most, if not all, of the students in the class participate by talking, in addition to listening to others.
- Students generally elaborate on their ideas and thinking in more than brief utterances of a few words.
- The proportion of time involving "student talk" versus "teacher talk" is at least 50 percent students to 50 percent teacher, but preferably 60 percent to 100 percent student talk.
- Students listen to and respond to each other's contributions and not only to the teacher.
- Students and teachers frequently engage in uptake in which they acknowledge their understanding or seek to clarify a speaker's point(s) by summarizing or restating it before responding to it.

The excerpts in Figures 5.2, 5.3, and 5.4 illustrate classroom discussions that fulfill the criteria for authentic discussion listed in Figure 5.1. In these excerpts, teachers prompt students to express their ideas and elaborate on them. They do not dominate or monopolize the dialogue. They work to make sure that the dialogue involves a wide number of students and that students respond to each other's comments. They focus on exploring genuine questions, avoiding any implication that a particular position is the "right" one or that they have a preference for a particular position or a predetermined answer.

Figure 5.2. Excerpts from a role-playing discussion.

[*Student Roles: Professor, Parent 1, Parent 2, Student at Millikan, Social Studies Instructor*]

MS. BREZEL: So the community school board meeting is now called to order. Please silence and put away all your electronic devices. Our first order listing tonight is the concern of the proposed curriculum at Millikan High School which includes the instruction on the concept of white privilege in eleventh-grade social studies classes. Please keep in mind that the goal of tonight's meeting is not to make a decision but to hear both sides and take those sides under consideration when the decision is made at a future date. The Board would like to take this opportunity to open the forum to those who are in favor of the proposed curriculum and to express their viewpoints. Considering the nature of this topic, the board insists that this discourse remain civil and respectful. Is there anyone at this point who is in favor of this curriculum that would like to go first? Thank you! And you are …

[In this role-playing discussion, the teacher plays a role along with the students.]

PROFESSOR: Professor.

MS. BREZEL: OK.

Figure 5.2. Continued

PROFESSOR: Oh, actually, Professor Akin. I like that better. I am in favor of it because I mean, it is life. Stuff happens. There is no way like of avoiding it. If you don't teach it, kids are going to find out eventually and they might find out in the wrong way and get the wrong ideas about it. That is all I see it. No. That is not like my idea.

[Student calls out]: You stay in the character.

MS. BREZEL: Thanks for your input, Professor.

PROFESSOR: You're welcome.

MS. BREZEL: Would anybody like to contribute to that? Or does anyone have . . . thank you. Yes. And you are . . .

PARENT 1: I am a professor parent.

MS. BREZEL: OK and also. Excellent. Thank you.

PARENT 1: If they get into the real world, they need to be taught. The only way to stop it or recognize it is actually that your kids realize what is going on. Otherwise, they are going to remain ignorant and blind.

[Speakers engage in the role-playing by stating their positions and providing support.]

[Student calls out]: I can't hear.

MS. BREZEL: I appreciate your [inaudible]. Is there anybody who likes to add to that?

PARENT 2: Could you restate what you were saying, please?

PARENT 1: I just said that we should educate kids about it otherwise it will become a problem and they won't really know about it. They won't know how to solve it or . . .

MS. BREZEL: Would you like to respond to that?
[The teacher encourages response by thanking speakers and asking students their views. She avoids evaluative responses such as "correct" or "I don't think that's right."]

PARENT 2: Oh, yeah.

MS. BREZEL: And you are . . .

PARENT 2: A parent that is against it. It is not something. It shouldn't be the subject that they learn. It is an unconscious thing that has been going on. Like white people [inaudible] like against minorities as a whole. You know, white privilege is the subject that is supposed be an unconscious thing that you get. I am not supposed to know that just because I am a black being followed in a grocery store or on the street that follows. I am not [inaudible] them. That is just something that just might be happen because of the [inaudible]. You are not going to be followed because you are white. That is like the subject, she was like "you cannot follow me because I am white." You know what I am saying, it shouldn't be something you need to know 'cause you don't . . . it is not like "are you racist?" No, right. It's not like you need to know what you can and what you can't do because of your color. You understand?

MS. BREZEL: If I may clarify, you are saying, if you don't know what is happening, you are better off not being aware of it?
[To encourage elaboration, the teacher uses uptake by stating—as a question—what the speaker has said.]

PARENT 2: Yeah, but it is like you know that you are going to get something and then like you know [unclear]. Like you know you can do these things without getting in trouble like or being caught. You may try to do it. I am not saying Lisa is going to do it because I mean, she does know lots of common sense. Like some other kids that are listening in a junior class [unclear]. They are not adults. They are still teenagers. So you know what I am saying? It

continued on next page

Figure 5.2. Continued

was like teaching them could be like a bad thing as well as it could be a bad thing to start it like he could argue against [inaudible]. Things could get . . . you know people are paying attention to that. Racism [unclear] like always the bad topic. You know what I am saying like [unclear].

[As a result of the teacher's uptake, the speaker elaborates in order to clarify and support the claim that was made.]

MS. BREZEL: Do you want to add to that at this point?

INSTRUCTOR: I am a social studies instructor. I am against it. I think that instead of teaching where we were going in this subject while everybody knows some stuff on the topic [unclear]. I think we should start from the base like color blindness. Just start out where everyone is equal and teach it from there as how we should treat each other and how everyone else should be treated.

MS. BREZEL: Is our alternative to the idea of white privilege, is more of a more inclusive community across the board?

INSTRUCTOR: Without going into the topic with [unclear].

[Later in the discussion . . .]

PARENT 2: Yeah. But teaching it in the class is a waste of resources and a waste of time and a waste of energy to teach something that shouldn't be claimed and that shouldn't be actually acknowledged if you are trying to be in an equal environment to make this, you know, together.

STUDENT: Because it would cause more conflict.

MS. BREZEL: So you are saying that teaching it will cause more conflict. You are . . .

[inaudible]

[The teacher frequently uses uptake to encourage speakers to elaborate.]

MS. BREZEL: So you are saying it would cause more conflict. In what way?

STUDENT: Like in the way the white kids even though they are not guilty at the moment, they are still guilty. They feel guilty about it. They knew that . . . they are falsely accused.

MS. BREZEL: The white students are?

STUDENT: Because there is unequal [unclear].

MS. BREZEL: So you are afraid it's going to cause animosity between the white students and the black students.

[After several minutes of discussion . . .]

INSTRUCTOR: Yeah. In that video we watched [inaudible]. She didn't ask to be treated differently, she was just treated differently. So it wasn't the [inaudible].

PARENT 2: So like being oblivious to it is like different from like no one should get it. [A comment that if they know about white privilege white people might take advantage of having it.]

MS. BREZEL: Once they are aware of that privilege, they might abuse the privilege? OK. People we haven't heard from.

STUDENT: I feel like if they are aware of the white privilege, they could stop it. I don't remember where it is, other people can put it into action when they see what is actually happening in other places.

MS. BREZEL: So awareness equals prevention or limitation?

INSTRUCTOR: I think that if you teach color blindness, it would prevent that while not showing the point of people get advantages. Just teach them not to do that stuff like preventing that idea.

Figure 5.3. Excerpt from a whole class debriefing.

MS. ZORBA: I want to hear from people who haven't had a chance to speak. Mark? [Talking to other students who want to speak] I'm going to let him speak. I'm going to start calling on people. Yeah. Mark?

[The teacher strives to be sure that all students are included in the discussion.]

MARK: I mean I get that school doesn't have a lot of people, a lot of [minority] students in there. I mean that shouldn't matter. If there're—, if some kids want to know [about white privilege], then let them know. If some kids don't want to know, then don't let—, they don't have to learn about it. And, like, I feel the people who would want to know are the people who would want to change it. Like do something about it, and stop this, or like stand up to someone who is being racist to another person. I mean I—. For me I feel like it would be a good thing to, like, teach it because, not only would it prevent it, but, like, it'll [pause] teach them more about, like their world and what they're going to be ready for once they leave—. Once they grow up and go to their future, they're going to know; they're going to have more experience on this, uh, than any other people.

MILO: Uh, this is not a—, it is not [indistinct]. It's like—. What Jay said earlier about how minorities are, like, small, uh, in school. I don't really think that's a bad thing because, like, if they teach about white privilege there, then the people who do have it, can, like, use it in a good way. Like in the video we watched how that lady's, uh, receptionist there—stepsister, sister-in-law! And, uh, how she knew she had the privilege, or white privilege, whatever, and she used it to help her stepsister. So, like, maybe we can teach it in that way and [they'll] know how they can use it in a good way.

[The speaker builds on the prior speaker's comments and provides an example to support his claim.]

MS. ZORBA: Jake, I know you have the [unclear]. Are you ready to say it? Guys, a lot of you are sitting there with your pen. And it's about to explode inside of you. I want to hear it. I want to hear people who haven't spoken yet. Fred, you've got a lot to say to the people next to you, what about your white privilege. Do you have an opinion on this issue about whether or not they should teach it?

FRED: No.

MS. ZORBA: You don't have any opinion? No. All right, too bad. [Laughter] What do you think, Elton?

MS. ZORBA: So, if I want to learn algebra, and nobody else wants to learn algebra, I should start a club? Algebra club? No one else has to study algebra?

[The teacher uses uptake by returning to a previous claim and turning it into a question to focus on a response that has not yet been examined.]

MARCIA: Algebra is used every day, like in everyday life.

MS. ZORBA: Oh, but we don't—, we don't encounter ...

[Students cross-talking]

MS. ZORBA: That's right because I don't encounter people of other cultures here?[Students cross-talking]

MS. ZORBA: Guys, I want you to think about this a little bit. Do we need to have an algebra club to do algebra? We're not going to teach algebra anymore because they don't want to learn it. It's pretty clear that nobody wants to learn algebra. Yeah, Jay.

JAY: In that video, the difference was that the two women were adults. And they know about—

MS. ZORBA: Guys, listen, please. Listen. What?

JAY: The difference was the other two women were adults. And, like, they know how to handle a situation, like, kind of [unclear] high school kids.

continued on next page

Figure 5.3. Continued

ALEX: OK, but, like, high school kids are like young adults, aren't they? So, if they know what they're doing at a young age, they're going to know what to do in old age?

[Students cross-talking]

MS. ZORBA: Friends, we're getting—. Listen to one another. Listen. This is good. Elie is waiting too. Go ahead, Elie.

ELIE: Wow. OK, like. If you teach it, like, when they're younger, then maybe—. Cause—, if you're teaching it to high school students, when they grow up, they're going to have to be the people that are grown. And they'll be in charge of the world. So, maybe the world will get better, and it won't have white privilege if you teach it to them now.

JAY: If you teach it to them, it might—. You don't have to teach it to them at all.

[Students cross-talking]

MS. ZORBA: Wait, wait. We have people who haven't spoken yet. Shh. I hear a voice I haven't heard before. Shh.

ASRA: If we don't teach it, then it can get, like, out of hand. But if we teach it at, like, a younger in age, everyone, like, can start, like, learning earlier like how we should, like, be [unclear]. And like, with future generations coming into high school, then, like it will just, like, be different.

[A speaker builds on a previous speaker's point.]

JORGE: What—. Like what Jay said about how, uh, if you don't teach, it's going to go away. It's like—.

[A speaker presents an opposing argument—that not teaching about white privilege will help eliminate it.]

JAY: I didn't say it was going away.

CARLOS: Well, like—. He said it's not going to come up or something like that, right? So, like—, that's like saying if you have an infection and you don't treat it, it's not—, it's just going to go away. It's going to get worse.

[A speaker summarizes a claim made by another speaker and argues against it.]

JAY: No. I'm saying, like, I think we should teach it, but not like teach it in general, like teach it in the school.

[Student calls out]: Why not?

JAY: Because it will get to a point that kids are going to take it too far.

[Student calls out]: Why? No one is saying, like, that they should teach it—.

JAY: It happens every day.

MS. ZORBA: Friends, I love hearing you, but I want you to listen to each other also. OK?

JEAN: I got one. [Class chatter.]

MS. ZORBA: Hold on, guys. Jean's been trying to speak for a while.

[Students cross talk]: Go ahead . . . go ahead . . . my bad. Go ahead. That's OK. No, that's good. Go ahead.

MS. ZORBA: I'm going to let Jean speak. Go ahead, Jean.

JEAN: OK. You know how everyone's saying, like, you should teach it, like, at a young age. Like, I don't think that really matters to you, like, if you have parents that are maladjusted, you go home every day, and to hear them say, "Hey," like, "I don't care what your school is teaching you." I mean, like you're, like—. If you're going to live here, you got to go by my rules, like, how I raise you. Everyone against—. Like, everyone goes home. I just think that it doesn't really matter if you tell them at a young age what [unclear]—. Like, they do their own computer; they do their own things. They don't [unclear]. That's it.

Figure 5.3. Continued

[A speaker summarizes arguments that have been made previously in the discussion and raises an argument against them.]

MS. ZORBA: Friends, we're working on this. It's working. We're getting there. Iris, got something to say?

IRIS: I feel like it's better to make kids aware now, like at, a younger age in middle school. And, like, even though you go home to your parent and they have diverse views on what you are and what you want [unclear]. I feel like it's better that we know what we want other than what your parents want.

[Students cross-talking]

MS. ZORBA: OK, friends, Jay's been really patient. We're going to let him speak. Sarah's been really patient, so we're going to let her speak. Just listen. Go. Go, go, Jay.

JAY: Yeah. I don't—. I don't think we should teach about white privilege. We should teach about not being racist. [A student calls out: "Yeah." Another student: "I agree."] You don't have to teach about how whites were dominant and not dominant or being oppressed. Teach about not being racists to each other. Correct? Instead of teaching, like, history or about how whites were treated better.

MS. ZORBA: OK, Sarah.

SARAH: I think one of the arguments that we read was that, um, that people will do, like, their own thing. And, like, it doesn't matter. But, like, we teach, like, somehow like, you can't teach students this young [about white privilege]. But honestly, like—. We teach, like—. We've been teaching about racism and how you, like, like are equal to one another since, um, fifth grade. And, like, that helped us to be the people we are, like, now, today, like, all of us aren't racists. It's like, um, if you teach, like, white privilege is, like, people can feel guilty. Like, like, like, lots of students will make each other feel guilty cause, like—. That's not, like, [unclear]. And like, I feel, like, no matter what you teach every student, they're going, like, do what they want [unclear]. Um, when we were like little kids, we were, as friends, we never—. We weren't aware of, like, racism stuff. So, we just went, like, to anyone that we thought was, like, fun or anyone that we liked, that we thought were nice. And we never were like, oh, that person's color until—, "I'm not chocolate," because we were like six. We were like, oh, that person's funny. I'm going to talk to them. Or we never really, like—. Cause like, um, "I don't like their race." And then when we grew up with them, we're still friends with them. But now that we're, like, aware of the world, and we have worries like school, and we have to get jobs and stuff, and then we start learning about this, it's, like, sad because you have friends that are, like, different colors. Like, they have to go through this stuff. Or you have, like, white friends, and if you teach white privilege, then you're kind of being racist towards white people now. It's kind of just like you can't put any race above the other one. You should just treat everyone equal.

[Speakers are summarizing and addressing each other's reasoning and providing elaborated responses with claims, evidence, and sometimes warrants.]

Figure 5.4. Excerpt from a whole class debriefing.

SARAH: But people will still do it. Like we, like we can't solve everyone. You can't brainwash everyone not to be racist. Like if we teach racism, if we teach racism isn't correct, it's going to be, be prevented, yes. But there's still a group of people that won't listen to it and won't want to listen to it. Like they won't—. They will still be racist.

MS. ZORBA: OK. We're going to go all around the room again. OK. Mark, then AJ, then Jay, then Nicole. Go.

continued on next page

Figure 5.4. Continued

MARK: I mean, sexism, you'll get, you'll get punished for it. You'll get locked up, whatever. And you get consequences during school, whatever. But racism, they don't say anything. They'll just say, oh, don't do that, or it affects one side more than the other, maybe. I mean there's really no point of bringing sexism into kind of, like, racism, cause racism you can, ah—, not racism, sexism you get, uh, penalized or punishment for what you did. Racism is just a simple talk and a warning after you do that, you get a minor consequence than sexism.
[Speakers present claims and provide support.]

Ms. Zorba: OK. Go.

AJ: Don't you think that our, like now, like, us hearing about it now, this is a different freaking generation than old [unclear], doing stuff to other kids? Like, we are different people. Like it may happen right now, but it can't happen in the future if we already know that.

MS. ZORBA: OK, Jay.
[The teacher makes sure students each get a chance to respond.]

JAY: Yeah, it's a big topic, but like—. It's a big topic, but again, like, [unclear].

NICOLE: Well, um, we were talking about, how like, not everyone will, like, um, follow the rules of that without thinking about it. There's always, like, um—, there'll always going to be, like, people that aren't going to go, like, do what they're supposed to. But that's just the world. Like, not everyone is [indistinct phrase].

CARLOS: To follow up with what Nicole said, I don't really get your point. Like, are you saying that because people aren't going to follow what they are being taught, we shouldn't teach at all? Like, so, we shouldn't teach about sexism or anything like that because not everyone's going to follow it, right? Is that what you said?
[A speaker uses uptake by stating the previous speaker's point and raising questions about it.]

NICOLE: I mean if it's already taught, and you're saying that, like, it doesn't happen, like, it doesn't happen now, but it still happens. Then what's going to happen when we teach racism, and we want to prevent it, but it still happens.
[The speaker responds by defending her claim.]

[Students in cross-talk]

CARLOS: It's still, it's still a problem that you have.

[Students in cross-talk]

MS. ZORBA: Friends, friends. Friends, this is very interesting. I hope that you can please keep listening to one another. Thank you.
[The teacher encourages students to listen to each other and thanks them for their participation.]

AJ: I feel like racism is everywhere. And you can't really walk away with—, from it and you have to, like, stop it eventually. Because it's happening to you, you have to stop it. But if it's like sexism, you pointed out, like, oh, if it's a husband starts being sexist with you, you can leave him or you can divorce him. And you don't have to stay with him. And if someone is being sexist towards you, you don't have to take that. But if someone is being racist, it's like everywhere. And you can't stop everyone unless you, like, you talk about it somewhere. With, like, a big group, you teach it; and you, like, preach it to everyone.
[Speakers grapple with an argument made by one of the speakers—that sexism is punished more than racism.]

Why a Theory of Discussion Matters

In addition to having a clear vision of what authentic discussion entails, the teachers we observed and interviewed also view authentic discussion as being essential for learning to interpret texts and to write for a variety of purposes and audiences.

In a previous study (Kahn, 1999), teachers who reported valuing discussion fell into two distinct groups in terms of their views of why authentic discussion matters. One group, similar to the teachers described in this book, considered authentic discussion—both small group and whole class—an essential activity for helping students to develop and expand their abilities to think critically; to interpret texts; to support their interpretations with evidence; to respond to different interpretations and viewpoints; and to write effectively in a variety of situations. The teachers in this group consider small group and whole class discussion as opportunities for students to practice and hone these literacy and critical thinking skills.

The other group expressed the view that in order to keep students' attention and interest, teachers need to use a variety of different types of instructional activities. Along with activities like videos, performance, and music, small group and whole class discussion provide a means for varying the approach used in the classroom to keep students' attention and interest. Teachers in this group were less concerned with evaluating discussions in terms of the percentage of time involving student talk versus teacher talk and the number of students participating. They tended to evaluate discussions in terms of the extent that students appear interested and are paying attention rather than "zoning out."

The teachers who view discussion as essential practice for developing literacy skills tend to work hard to figure out ways to make discussions work so authentic discussions occur on a regular basis in their classrooms. When discussions do not proceed as they had hoped, they strategize about what they can do to make them better. They engage in an ongoing process of refining their own practices in guiding discussions and in helping students become more adept participants in discussions. In this chapter, we will examine some of the ways they work on honing their practice.

Establishing a Safe, Respectful Space for Discussion

The teachers we observed and interviewed all commented on the importance of establishing a classroom environment in which students feel comfortable and "safe" expressing their views—especially when confronting controversial issues. Ms. Widerhaken talked about working to create a "family atmosphere" in her classroom. Ms. Zorba described working to maintain a "respectful" environment among students.

When asked about how they go about establishing this kind of safe environment, the teachers were unanimous in emphasizing that it is crucial that they "know their students." They also say that it is important for students to get to know each other. Ms. Zorba and Ms. Widerhaken both advocate using interviewing activities early in the year. These activities involve students in interviewing each other and often in sharing what they learn with the entire class. Ms. Zorba described her approach as doing "a lot of observing and listening" to students (especially when they are working in pairs or small groups) to learn about their personalities.

Some of the teachers also used student surveys and/or questionnaires to learn about their students' interests, preferences, and feelings. Burke (2013) provides a sample of the kind of questionnaire teachers might design to learn about their students. Students might be asked questions such as the following:

- In what school or out-of-school activities and/or athletics are you involved?
- What kinds of things do you like to do in your free time?
- What kinds of things do you like to read?
- What are some recent movies you like?
- What music do you listen to?
- Where have you traveled recently?
- What kinds of activities do you like to do in English class? What do you dislike doing?
- What other information would you like me to know or understand about you?

Teachers should, of course, use what they know about their school and community to determine the most helpful and appropriate questions to ask in a student interest survey.

Another aspect of creating a safe classroom is establishing shared norms and expectations that focus on being respectful toward others. Sometimes teachers may present and explain norms that they expect students to follow. Even better

Figure 5.5. Sample classroom norms.

- Be kind to everyone.
- Treat everyone (yourself, classmates, teachers, and visitors) with respect.
- Respect your environment and the property of others.
- Keep hands, feet, and objects to yourself.

may be the approach of guiding students in developing their own norms. Figure 5.5 presents a sample set of norms that might be used with students. One other variation is that a set of norms like this could be presented to students with the goal of having them adapt or modify them for their own class.

Valuing Authentic Discussion

A commitment to authentic discussion as an essential activity for literacy learning means that authentic discussion is valued in the same way that English language arts teachers value literature, reading, and writing. For Ms. Torino, recognizing the value of authentic discussion means that it should be assessed and "counted" in evaluating student learning in the same ways as we assess and "count" students' performance in literary analysis, interpretation of texts, and writing. She explains that in activities such as arguing one's position in a gateway activity, students are repeatedly and frequently practicing and performing complex skills such as making claims, supporting claims by citing relevant evidence, providing warrants, and addressing counterclaims and counterevidence—and they are doing so probably more often than is possible in written work that is assessed by the teacher.

One way to value authentic discussion is through the use of a rubric for assessing participation in authentic discussion (see Figure 5.6). Students can use the rubric to assess their own participation in a discussion. Teachers might ask them to submit their own self-assessment and to include goals for themselves for the next discussion. Teachers can use the rubric to provide frequent and ongoing feedback to students about their participation in discussion and as a basis for "standards-based assessments" of student learning and growth in terms of discussion participation. In addition, providing students with a rubric, or co-creating a rubric together with students, helps them in understanding the protocols and expectations for participation in authentic discussion.

Figure 5.6. Assessing participation in authentic discussion.

	1	2	3
Finding evidence in the text(s)	I have the text(s) open on my desk.	I have the text(s) open, and I look up quotations that are referenced by others.	In addition to 1 and 2, I make references to specific textual quotations by page number.
Using evidence to support claims	Occasionally I use evidence to support claims.	Most of the time I use evidence and reasoning to support claims.	I almost always use relevant evidence and reasoning to support claims.
Listening respectfully	I listen respectfully to others.	I listen respectfully to others and sometimes make eye contact with the speaker(s).	I listen respectfully to others and almost always make eye contact with the speaker(s).
Using uptake (uptake = stating or summarizing what someone else has said before adding your own ideas)	At least once, I use uptake in responding to others' ideas.	I sometimes use uptake in responding to others' ideas.	I almost always use uptake in responding to others' ideas.
Encouraging others and a variety of viewpoints	I am attentive to the comments of others.	I encourage others to join the discussion.	I directly ask others questions or for their responses to ideas.

Teaching Students Protocols for Participating in Authentic Discussion

The teachers in this study were asked whether students enter their classes at the beginning of the year used to participating in authentic discussions in previous classes. The teachers said that they approach the year with the assumption that students are not used to doing so, explaining that in their experience it would be a mistake to assume that students know the protocols for engaging in authentic discussion. Their sense is that in general most of their students have not previously been in classes that frequently engaged in authentic discussion. As a result, they stated that they know they need to develop a plan to help students learn how to participate in discussion.

Of the teachers in this study, Ms. Torino appeared to design and implement the most extensive preparation for her students. She devotes time at the beginning of the year to having students practice authentic discussion using a series of scaffolded activities. Several specific protocols that Ms. Torino wants students to learn are the following:

- Speakers quote from or identify specific evidence from the focal texts.
- Speakers explain what quotes or evidence show and why.
- Speakers use uptake, restating or summarizing a previous speaker.
- After responding, speakers call on the next person to speak, making sure first to call on others who have not yet responded or not recently responded (if everyone has participated).

Ms. Torino has students participate in a series of small group and whole class discussions to practice these protocols. For example, students might work on practicing uptake by discussing a scenario, such as the scenario in Figure 5.7, in small groups and then whole class discussion. Students might be asked to focus on using uptake by summarizing or paraphrasing what another student has said before expressing their own views on the issue. For example, in discussing the scenario in Figure 5.7, a student might say, "I think it's right to stand up for what you believe in and that's what the editor did." Another student responds, "Angela says it was right because the student editor stood up for what she believes in. I agree, but other people, like the athlete, are also standing up for what they believe in, so they're right too. I think everyone has the right to express their belief, so maybe the editor should state in the newspaper what the athlete says about 'Redskins,'" and so on.

After students have participated in discussions, small group or whole class, Ms. Torino reports that she involves students in a debriefing or postmortem session in which they evaluate how effective the discussion was, what weaknesses there were, and how they could make it better. One way to approach a debriefing would be to have students use the rubric (see Figure 5.6) to evaluate their

Figure 5.7. Practicing protocols for authentic discussion.

High school officials disciplined the student editor and faculty adviser of the student newspaper after the paper refused to print the word *Redskins*, the nickname (mascot) of the school, saying the word is offensive. The school principal indefinitely suspended the student editor from the newspaper and suspended the faculty adviser from school without pay for two days. The principal opposed the newspaper's ban on the word, saying that it violated the First Amendment rights of those who wanted to use the word because it is the school's nickname. A student athlete stated, "When I'm playing hard for our team to win, I'm thinking, 'Win this for the Redskins!' which motivates me to do my best, so how can the school newspaper reject the mascot? The newspaper should have pride in our teams and our mascot." The student editor and faculty adviser believe that their punishment was unfair. *Were the student editor and/or faculty adviser right or wrong to disobey school officials? Was their punishment fair? Did the school officials act appropriately? Explain why or why not.*

own participation. In critiquing discussions, students may also point out shortcomings such as some students tended to dominate, at one point comments got sidetracked on a tangent, or sometimes people took turns presenting different viewpoints but did not really ever address points that others made (more of a "round-robin" turn-taking format). It's important to note that as students are learning to participate in authentic discussion, a round-robin format in which each participant takes a turn stating his or her ideas and evidence may be a good starting place. It is an approach that encourages each student to participate and can keep the conversation from becoming teacher centered or teacher dominated. Students can subsequently work on summarizing and then adding to, qualifying, or disagreeing with specific ideas raised by others.

Ms. Torino also suggested the use of written transcripts of student discussions as useful in postmortems. If a discussion is audio-recorded, software can be used to expedite transcription. Teachers can guide students in discussing the transcripts as texts, analyzing the specific moves that were made in the discussion and their effects, and talking about what might have been said that wasn't.

To help teachers and students conduct postmortem analyses of discussions, Dawn Forde from Adlai E. Stevenson High School in Lincolnshire, Illinois (Kahn, McCann, Walter, Bouque, & Forde, 2017), has used an app that allows the teacher to input a seating chart and track discussion from participant to participant, identifying the person-to-person flow of the conversation. The outcome of the tracking is an overall diagram of the flow of the discussion that teacher and students can then analyze for patterns and trends. Apps that can be used for this purpose are "Equity Maps—Classroom, Groups, and Meetings" by David Nelson and "Round Table—Harkness Discussion Tracking" by Nicolas Madole. See Figure 5.8 for an example of a chart tracking a discussion.

Integrating Authentic Discussion Frequently throughout the Year

Another aspect of valuing authentic discussion means making it a regular and frequent feature of instruction throughout the year. Incorporating authentic discussion—both small group and whole class—involves setting aside the time to teach students protocols and to engage students in discussion on a regular basis and not just occasionally as a change of pace. Teachers who believe in the importance of authentic discussion to students' literacy learning make it a priority and tend not to jettison discussion activities to "cover" more material.

Figure 5.8. Tracking the flow of discussion.

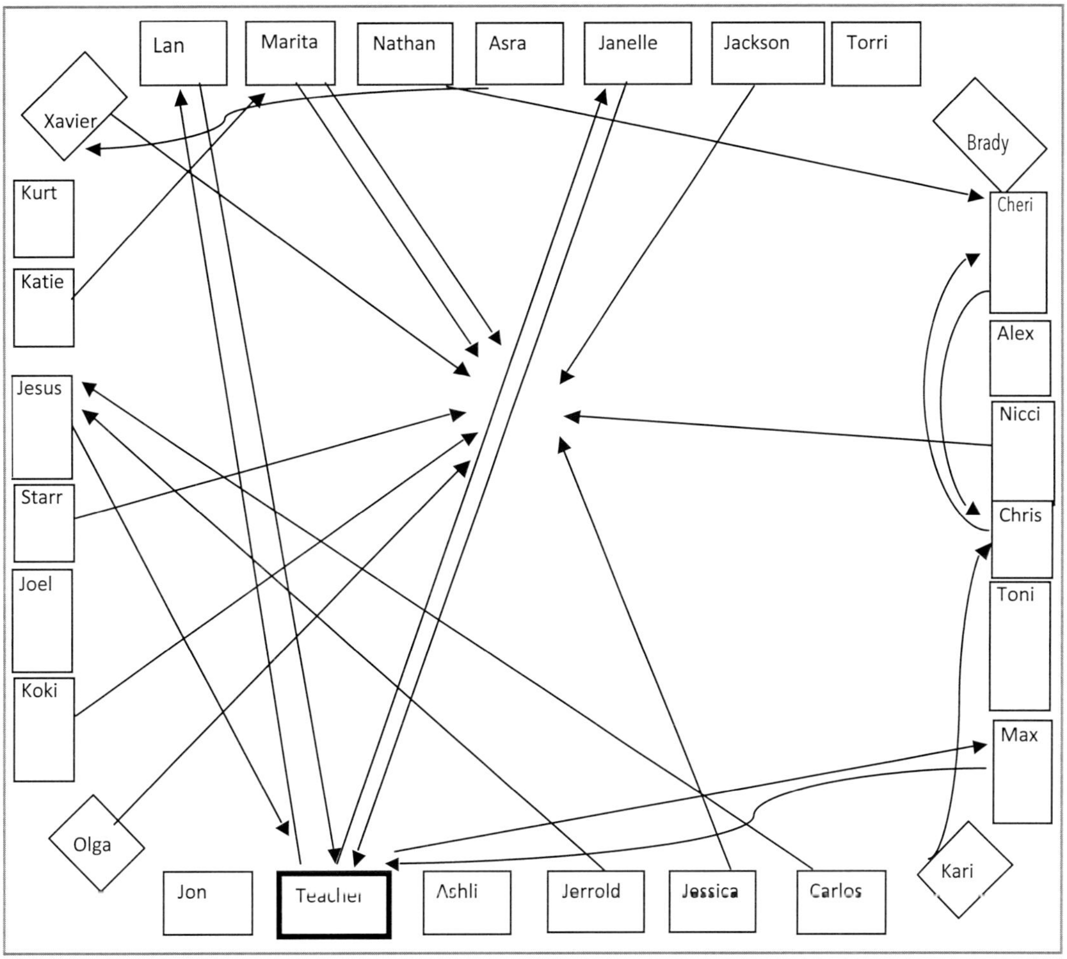

Arranging Seating to Enhance Authentic Discussion

Part of creating an environment for authentic discussion involves thinking about the arrangement of the classroom. Authentic discussion can be enhanced (or inhibited) as a result of the way students and teachers are positioned. We have found that when students are discussing in small groups the optimum size is generally three to five students per group. Sometimes it makes sense to use pairs for discussion. If students are in individual desks, they need to be taught routines for moving their desks into tight circles to facilitate discussion. The groups need to be spaced out around the room so they do not distract each other. If possible, it works well for groups to meet at separate tables around the room. In the classes we observed, the teachers circulated as students worked in small groups, listening in on conversations and occasionally joining a group for a few minutes to answer questions or to redirect the group if needed.

For whole class discussion, a seating arrangement in which students can look directly at each other seems to work best, such as a circle or a horseshoe. A seating arrangement with students in traditional rows all facing the front of the room is problematic for authentic discussion since students are all looking at the teacher rather than at each other. The arrangement discourages students from using uptake and responding to each other rather than mostly to the teacher. We have seen some classes have two or three rows of students on each side of the room with each side facing the other and the center of the room, or there is a double or triple semicircle. These configurations are more conducive to discussion than rows all facing the front of the room but not as ideal as a circle or horseshoe, since students will have their backs to some, although not to as many, of the other students.

Another possibility is a fishbowl arrangement with an inner circle and an outer circle. In using a fishbowl, students in the inner circle are engaged in discussion while those in the outer circle observe and take notes. Then the students in the outer circle move to the inner circle to take their turn discussing and the students in the inner circle move to the outer circle. A variation is giving students in the outer circle the opportunity to "tap in" to the inner circle when they would like to engage in the dialogue (the tapped student moves to the other student's seat in the outer circle). To lessen disruption, students are usually limited to tapping in one at a time.

In the whole class discussions we observed, teachers often sat in a desk in the circle along with the students, or when students themselves were running the discussion, they sometimes sat behind or outside of the student circle. With these arrangements, teachers suggested that they wanted to be considered equal participants along with students or were primarily observers. Some of the teachers stood during whole class discussions, but instead of standing at one place such as in the front of the room, they tended to be moving around to different areas of the room. Through their movement to different areas, they tended to indirectly encourage students to look at and respond to each other and not to look just at the teacher. See Figure 5.9 for a summary of ways to encourage participation.

Figure 5.9. How do teachers create an environment for authentic discussion?

Teachers work with their students to

- Establish a safe, respectful space in which everyone knows each other well
- Agree on norms for collaborating with each other
- Develop standards and expectations for how to engage in authentic discussion
- Value authentic discussion by assessing it and "counting" it in similar ways as other aspects of literacy learning (such as writing) are assessed and counted
- Teach and practice protocols for engaging in authentic discussion
- Arrange classroom seating to enhance authentic discussion

Igniting and Sustaining Authentic Discussion

Creating a classroom environment that is conducive to authentic discussion is crucial, but equally important is the design of the inquiry and the instructional activities and materials that are the basis for discussion. The earlier chapters have explored how instructional activities can be designed to provide the basis for engaging students in inquiry, discussion, and writing. An intriguing issue or problem, along with data and human or emotional connections, is key to igniting discussion. After students in this study read the article about some parents who complained about a social studies class in which students were learning about the concept of white privilege, examined information about what was included in the classroom instruction, and watched a video revealing a situation in which a store clerk treated a person who was white one way and a person of color another way (see pp. 132–40), students were anxious to talk about the issues. But once students have ideas they want to talk about, what do teachers do to ensure that the discussion that is sparked grows and does not fizzle out prematurely?

Avoiding Any Suggestion of Having a Preferred Position or Viewpoint

If the teachers that we observed had a particular viewpoint on the gateway cases and issues, they gave absolutely no indication of it. They also explained to students that there was not one "right" position and that the goal is to consider different viewpoints and the strengths and weaknesses of various arguments so they gain a greater understanding of the issues. At least one of the teachers involved students in discussing the effects and possible benefits of examining different perspectives on a controversy such as teaching about white privilege in high school social studies classes or a school purchasing robot teachers.

Using Uptake to Encourage Student Elaboration

When students presented their views or responded to others, the teachers maintained their "neutrality" by generally avoiding suggesting that their responses were "right" or "good." Sometimes the teachers didn't respond at all but instead looked intently at students who were speaking, exhibiting facial expressions that communicated attentiveness and interest. Sometimes they thanked students for sharing their ideas. In the excerpt in Figure 5.2, Ms. Brezel says, "Thanks for your input, Professor," and later, "Thank you." In the excerpt in Figure 5.4, Ms. Zorba rarely comments on student responses but instead concentrates on making sure all students get a chance to speak ("OK. We're going to go all around the room again. OK. Mark, then AJ, then Jay, then Nicole. Go."). Students were often so eager to speak that she had to remind them to listen to each other and that everyone would have a chance to be heard. At one point she says, "Friends, friends. Friends, this is very interesting. I hope that you can please keep listening to one another. Thank you."

Often if teachers suggest to students that their response is "good," "correct," or "right," it may have the effect of ending further dialogue: Presumably if the right answer has been given, then there is nothing else to say. Using uptake is a way to encourage students to say more. Uptake for teachers involves restating what a student has said and making the response a question. It is a good way to check that you have correctly understood the student and also to encourage further elaboration.

In the excerpt in Figure 5.2, Ms. Brezel uses uptake several times. For example, a student ends her comments saying, "It's not like you need to know what you can and what you can't do because of your color." Ms. Brezel says, "If I may clarify, you are saying, if you don't know what is happening, you are better off not being aware of it?" The student (Parent 2) responds, "Yeah, but it is like you know that you are going to get something and then like you know [unclear]. Like you know you can do these things without getting in trouble like or being caught. You may try to do it. I am not saying Lisa is going to do it because I mean, she does know lots of common sense. . . ." Ms. Brezel's use of uptake prompts the student to elaborate on her original claim.

At another point, a student says that teaching about white privilege will cause more conflict. Ms. Brezel responds using uptake, "So you are saying it would cause more conflict. In what way?" The student replies, "Like in the way the white kids even though they are not guilty at the moment, they are still guilty. They feel guilty about it. They knew that . . . They are falsely accused." By using uptake themselves, teachers model for students how this conversational move functions in discussion.

Inviting Response Rather Than Interrogating

At times teachers may need to be more direct in guiding the discussion. However, the teachers we observed did so by being invitational rather than interrogational or inquisitional (Walsh, 2017). They stated questions in such a way as to suggest they see some contradictions or are confused about the implications of an idea rather than that they are criticizing or attacking the idea. For example, in Ms. Zorba's class at one point most students seemed to be convinced by the argument that only students who wanted to learn about white privilege should have to do so. She redirected the discussion by saying, "Guys, I want you to think about this a little bit. Do we need to have an algebra club to do algebra? We're not going to teach algebra anymore because they don't want to learn it. It's pretty clear that nobody wants to learn algebra. Yeah, Jay?"

We have found that if students are not addressing an important counterargument or counterevidence, it is sometimes helpful for teachers to redirect the discussion by playing devil's advocate. In our experience, however, if the teacher actually plays the advocate for a certain viewpoint ("Isn't it better for students to learn about white privilege in a school setting where potential conflicts and resentments can be addressed in a supportive environment?"), some students may assume this viewpoint is what the teacher actually thinks and believes is right. An alternative approach—that has less potential for being misunderstood—is to refer students to what someone in one of the roles has said. ("But what about the counselor who says that it is better for students to learn about white privilege in a school setting where potential conflicts and resentments can be addressed in a supportive environment? How would you respond to that?") Or another move is to say, "Some people say. . . ."

It may also be necessary in some situations to review facts of the case. Perhaps there is confusion among students about what happened. Or maybe there is some information in the case materials that students appear to have missed.

This could be a situation where teachers feel that more of a recitation-style questioning approach is appropriate. However, we have found that even in this situation, teachers can create a more authentic conversation than is typical in recitation. Here's a possible way to proceed. The teacher says to the class that it seems it might be helpful at this point to review the information in the case and the facts before us. She asks, "Who will start us out with something that happens in the case?" As a student responds, the teacher jots a brief note of what is said on the board or on the computer, projected for the class to see. She continues to solicit input from many students about additional important information ("What else happened?," "What happened before that?," "What happened next?," or "Why was that important?" and so forth). The idea is to review the case in an open-ended way by encouraging input from many different students. Occasionally, misinformation will be recorded, but we have found that after a few minutes students will point out that something listed is not correct and we can then make necessary revisions without directly telling a student that he or she is incorrect. When students correct information that is written on the board or screen, it is less threatening because they have often forgotten who it was that provided the information.

Being Patient: Trusting Students and the Inquiry Process

In the classrooms that we observed, sometimes students expressed unclear logic, struggled with concepts (such as the meaning of *white privilege*), or pursued questionable arguments (such as the idea that it is better for people to remain ignorant of a social injustice so that they don't feel bad about being treated unfairly). But rather than quickly jumping in to rescue, the teachers gave their students time and space to try to work out their thinking. They trusted that through the discussion students would refine and clarify their thinking and would work through their confusion. They let students "try out" arguments to see how they were received. One of Ms. Zorba's students eventually addresses the argument that if some students don't want to learn about white privilege they shouldn't have to, by saying,

> I don't really think that's a bad thing because, like, if they teach about white privilege there, then the people who do have it, can, like, use it in a good way. Like in the video we watched how that lady's, uh, receptionist there—stepsister, sister-in-law! And, uh, how she knew she had the privilege, or white privilege, whatever, and she used it to help her stepsister. So, like, maybe we can teach it in that way and [they'll] know how they can use it in a good way.

Troubleshooting

What do teachers do when discussion isn't working? What if students are hesitant to talk and don't participate? We've often heard teachers lament, "Trying to have a discussion today was like pulling teeth." Our interviews revealed several things that the teachers we observed do when students are not participating. Again, we need to stipulate that first teachers need to provide students with material worthy of inquiry by developing a case that is likely to stimulate discussion and that contains enough meat to give students much to contemplate and deliberate about, such as the gateway activities described in previous chapters. But sometimes even the best of activities does not immediately lead to lively participation.

These are recommendations from the teachers interviewed:

- *Have students work in small groups before participating in whole class discussion.* The construction of the gateway activities involves students in planning what their character in the role-playing forum will say. They have a chance to try out claims, evidence, and warrants; to rehearse and refine their arguments; and to think about how they can address counterarguments and/or counterevidence. They are not asked to enter the whole class discussion cold; they have contributions ready to present. Small group discussions can be a way to prepare students for participating in whole class discussion and allow them to feel more confident in expressing themselves.
- *Have students individually write briefly about their response to the question(s) for discussion before starting a whole class discussion.* Then one way to launch the whole class discussion is to have a few students report what they have written. Their responses are likely to motivate others to begin responding as well.
- *Directly ask students what they think about the case while communicating a sincere desire to know their views.* Again, the key is having an invitational tone and approach.
- *Be alert or sensitive to the possibility that something may have happened in school or in the community that is concerning students more than the activity at hand.* This is a point when the teachers say it is important to know their students and to have established relationships so students feel comfortable sharing concerns.

On the other hand, the problem may be that students all talk at once, interrupt others, become too verbally aggressive, and do not listen to each other.

Ms. Zorba commented that this is a situation that she thinks is actually not so problematic or difficult to manage. She says that the eagerness of many students to speak at once means that they are interested and enthusiastic, which she considers a good thing. Her job then is to assure students that everyone will get a chance to participate, to orchestrate turn-taking, and to make sure everyone politely listens to each other and gives others a chance to speak without interruption. The excerpt in Figure 5.3 shows examples of Ms. Zorba dealing with students who are sometimes talking over each other and trying to get into the dialogue without listening to others. For example, at one point Ms. Zorba says, "OK, friends, Jay's been really patient. We're going to let him speak. Sarah's been really patient, so we're going to let her speak. Just listen. Go. Go, go, Jay."

Honing the Art and Craft of Authentic Discussion

Using authentic discussion in the classroom is an ongoing process—for both students and teachers. Every attempt will not result in the desired outcomes. For teachers the process involves continual reflection and analysis: What went well, what didn't, what could or should I have done differently? Figure 5.10 offers a summary of ways to keep a discussion *authentic*.

The rubric "Teacher Self-Evaluation of Discussion" (Figure 5.11) provides a basis for self-evaluation and reflection about the strengths of a specific discussion and how it could be improved. It provides a road map of specific aspects to examine in evaluating discussions and goals to set for future discussions. It is often helpful for teachers to video-record discussions so that there is the opportunity to go back and reflect on what occurred. Given everything that is going on in a discussion, all the decisions that are involved, and the array of details that teachers have to attend to at once, it is often difficult to recall everything that happened or to remember events accurately. A video recording provides an opportunity to step back and look at everything with fresh eyes removed from the challenges and pressures of the moment.

Figure 5.10. Keeping a discussion going: What do teachers do?

- They avoid leading students to think they have a preferred position or viewpoint.
- They use uptake in responding to students, instead of praise such as "right" or "good answer."
- They invite response rather than interrogating students.
- They show patience as students grapple with issues, trusting students and the inquiry process.
- They have strategies for dealing with complications, such as students being hesitant to talk or not listening to each other.

Figure 5.11. Teacher self-evaluation of discussion.

	1	2	3
Creating a respectful, safe space	I exhibited rapport with the class in general, and they generally listened to each other.	I exhibited rapport with most students, and they usually listened respectfully to each other's views.	I exhibited rapport with all students, and they listened attentively and respectfully to each other's views.
Teaching the protocols of authentic, dialogic discussion	I previously presented students with the protocols of authentic, dialogic discussion.	I involved students previously in developing and practicing the protocols of authentic, dialogic discussion.	I previously scaffolded a series of activities to engage students in practicing and refining the protocols of authentic, dialogic discussion.
Promoting inquiry rather than indoctrination	I attempted to be "invitational" in questioning and responding to students, rather than "inquisitional" or "interrogational."	Most of the time, I was "invitational" in questioning and responding to students, rather than "inquisitional" or "interrogational."	My questioning, responses, and tone were always "invitational" rather than "inquisitional" or "interrogational."
Staying on task	There were some off-task responses by students.	There were few off-task responses by students.	There were very few or no off-task responses by students.
Using uptake (uptake = stating or summarizing what someone else has said to encourage students to elaborate and to encourage response without suggesting a response is right or wrong)	A few times, I used uptake during the discussion.	I used uptake several times in responding to students' ideas.	I almost always used uptake in responding to students' ideas.
Encouraging response from all students	At least half of the students responded at least one time. I mostly avoided having a few students dominate the discussion.	About 75% of the students responded at least one time. I avoided having a few students dominate the discussion.	All of the students responded at least one time. I avoided having a few students dominate the discussion.
Monitoring the percentage of student talk versus teacher talk	At least 50% of the "talk time" was student talk as opposed to teacher talk.	At least 65% of the "talk time" was student talk.	80%–100% of the "talk time" was student talk.
Monitoring students' elaboration	Student responses were often more than one sentence in length.	Student responses generally were elaborated and involved at least a few sentences.	Students often explained their thinking at length in several sentences.
Monitoring students' use of uptake	Students responded to each other (not just the teacher) and occasionally used uptake.	Students often responded to each other's ideas and used uptake in about half of their responses.	Students mostly responded to each other's ideas and frequently used uptake.
Connecting the discussion to ongoing inquiry and writing	I explained to students how the discussion connects to an ongoing inquiry and writing.	I engaged students in explaining how the discussion connects to an ongoing inquiry and writing.	Students made numerous connections within the discussion to ongoing inquiry, as well as making connections within their writing.

6 The Follow-Through: Coherence, Sustained Inquiry, and Flexibility

The teachers in our study engaged students in substantive discussions about complex problems fostered by an array of strategies and techniques. Earlier research reports that students who engaged in extended discussions on a topic of inquiry not only learned content but also practiced procedural strategies important to developing both oral and written argument. These students evaluated examples, scanned a variety of opinions, recognized and responded to challenges to their conclusions, gave claims [reasons] in support of their opinions, and buttressed their reasons with examples and interpretations (McCann, 2014, pp. 97–98). As noted in our review of research in Chapter 1, a substantial body of research identifies the connection between frequent classroom discussions and measures of literacy learning and achievement.

As substantive as they were, the discussions in our study were not an end in themselves. Their extension into processes for written responses and extensions into longer lines of inquiry are the final desired outcome. We see promise in the cases of teachers who were able to plan and facilitate a series of discussions that learners found consequential. The discussions that we observed in five different high schools were not isolated and rare experiences. For the teachers whom we observed, discussion about substantive issues and complex themes was the primary mode of instruction, and all ended in substantive writing.

In this chapter, we report and explore

- how students' discussions linked to students' writing;
- how the discussions about specific cases connected students to other discussions about texts;
- how teachers have used discussions about complex and sometimes emotional issues as a means for introducing a line of inquiry or as a way to foster reflection about learning;
- how teachers can link together several discussions, supported by the critical examination of various texts, across a program of inquiry on broader but related themes that extends across several weeks of classes; and
- how teachers can incorporate examinations of white privilege into the texts they teach.

Developing Opinions in Writing

First, the students' written responses that followed discussions allowed the teachers to judge the benefits of the discussions, students' understanding of the complex issues and the related texts, and students' command of procedures for arguing for a policy position. Teachers using the case studies for the Robot Teacher and Teaching about White Privilege asked students to clarify and develop their own opinions in written responses that took the form of letters to school boards stating their respective opinions on the issue at hand. In Chapter 2 we share the Robot Teacher writing prompt and a sample of a student's response. Following the two days of discussion about the Teaching about White Privilege case, the students we observed were given the following prompt for written responses:

> Write a letter to the Board of Education of Hope to convince them of your viewpoint on the issue of whether eleventh-grade social studies classes at Millikan High School should include instruction on the concept of white privilege. Provide specific supporting evidence for your viewpoint.
>
> Your letter will need to
>
> - Introduce and explain the issue that you are writing about
> - Provide specific evidence and reasoning to support your viewpoint
> - Provide a response to arguments and evidence in opposition to (against) your viewpoint

One student letter in response to this prompt argued that a "white privilege" curriculum should not be taught at Millikan High School:

> **Sample Student Response to Controversy Regarding Teaching about White Privilege**
>
> Dear Superintendent,
>
> I believe that "white privilege" should not be a required portion of the curriculum for a variety of reasons. For starters, it creates racial tension between the students and it makes white students feel guilty while making the non-whites, mostly African Americans, feel uncomfortable. Teaching white privilege would make problems worse instead of solving them. White privilege is a very opinion-based topic and could not only make problems worse, but also create new ones. Keep in mind that I am white and I grew up in a very diverse neighborhood and school district.

In behalf of creating racial tension, I have a personal experience to share. About three years ago, I was in seventh grade. One friend of mine, who rode the bus home with me was African-American. During this time, we had assigned seats on the bus and everyone knew that. Everyone wanted to sit in the back because it was "cool" and it just so happened that my friend and I luckily got the last seat in the back of the bus. After school that day we started climbing the stairs of the bus to see a white boy in our seat. My friend had asked him if he could move and he stared at him and replied, "Didn't you pay attention to the history lesson today? White's are allowed to take black's seats." If it isn't obvious, we had been talking about Rosa Parks and the bus boycott. The only reason I remember this was because he then proceeded to say "what are you going to do? Boycott the bus?" Although the white boy had never mentioned anything about fighting, it provoked it. My African-American friend then approached the kid and repeatedly punched him in the face, all because the lesson had been mentioned in the wrong way. Teaching things that prove whites have more rights than non-whites could be taught in such a wrong way that provokes the high school students even more than the junior high students because they are exposed to violence more. Racial tension and violence exposure are not a good combination.

In addition to making the students mad, it can make them sad. For example, white students will feel guilty. It will be made a point that it is all white people's fault that nonwhites are not treated fair. Some whites discriminate, but not all. There is no need to make the white students that include people of all races in activities feel guilty. An unnamed parent interviewed by Fox News emphasizes how white students will feel: "They're teaching white guilt. They're dividing the students. They're saying to nonwhites, 'You have been oppressed and you're still being oppressed'" ('White Privilege' Lesson in Delavan-Darien High School Class in Wisconsin Draws Ire'). This guilt that whites will feel will divide the students because they will feel like other races don't like them and that it is bad to be white. Being a white student in high school, I know how teens will react. They would turn to whites and say "this is all your fault!" Joking or not, it can still make the whites feel at fault. I know I would feel guilty and upset that people think it's my fault that the world isn't united as a whole because of segregation. Although some whites discriminate, the ones that don't get a bad reputation throughout the world because all whites are included when talking about the bad things that have been done. Some non-white people discriminate against whites too but they aren't thought of as racists. People act like whites don't face struggles of feeling segregated. Maybe we don't feel as bad as nonwhites, but that doesn't mean it's okay to treat us badly due to our skin color either.

Furthermore, not only does it make whites feel bad about themselves, but it makes people of races besides white feel uncomfortable. For example, during my English class, we had a discussion about white privilege. And one African-American student calmly raised her hand and said: "Look around. I'm the only black person in this class. Not everyone is white, some are Hispanic but it still doesn't matter because you guys have someone of the same race to relate to." My teacher had then said "In other words, you feel uncomfortable discussing this in the class because you're the only African-American and feel like no one else relates to you?" She had confirmed with him that that is what she meant and he sincerely understood. Imagine this was a teacher who didn't understand that she felt uncomfortable, and told her to get over it because it's a class discussion and it's about races as a whole and not just her. Can you even imagine how she would feel? This uncomfortable feeling may or may not have been lifted off her shoulder when the bell rang. It could have followed her through the halls the whole day, making her look at every white person she walked past and feel different and unwanted due to her skin color. This also could have made her look at white people differently and sparked a hatred that she feels toward them. That whole feeling is just so unnecessary and excessive and leads to a division.

All in all, I still stand to say that white privilege should not be an obligatory aspect of the high school curriculum. It will create racial tension, and divide the students by making whites feel guilty and non-whites uncomfortable. In my opinion, "white privilege" doesn't exist. People will complain that they will be followed around by security guards in stores because they're black. And I think they're wrong because presentation is the key. If a white person walked in a store with dark glasses, a hat that covered their face, and their hands in their pocket, they would be followed by security too. Barak Obama is black, and he is one of the most successful men in the world. So I believe everything happens because of the way you present yourself to the public, and race has nothing to do with how successful you can be, or whether or not people think you are dangerous.

Sincerely,
Alexa

In her letter, the writer states reasons for her position and develops them from cited secondary sources as well as personal experience, including a recent one in her classroom. Affirming the significance of uptake, the student in her fourth paragraph cites an example of her teacher's uptake to a student's response during discussion: "In other words, you feel uncomfortable discussing this in the class because you're the only African-American and feel like no one else relates to you?" According to the writer's analysis, the teacher's response made the African American student feel valued and heard. Her argument not only privileged the teacher's response but also acknowledged that not every teacher would be as well equipped to handle the discussion, making it potentially uncomfortable or unproductive.

In accord with McCann's (2014) report regarding the close connection between extended discussions and elaborated writing, students at Stonebridge High School directly referenced classroom discussions in their letters written to the Hope School Board. For example, during the first day of discussion, the student portraying the school security guard identified as African American, in her role as well as in real life, and hypothesized being exposed to white privilege lessons as a student at Millikan. Arguing against its inclusion in the curriculum, she declared, "So if I was in this class, we already had to hear about us being in slavery. We already had to hear about getting beat and all that. So why would I want to hear about me not being able to be walking on the street without getting shot? Why would I have to hear, just because I am black, I have to have a Link card or just because I am black, I don't have long hair or I can't have a big house and I can't have a nice car. Why do I have to constantly be hearing that?"

In his letter to the Hope School Board, a student from Stonebridge High School referenced this sentiment in an extended argument in support of the opinion that the curriculum should not be taught due to the topic's extreme sensitivity:

Student Letter Excerpt

White privilege is a very sensitive topic, not just sensitive but highly emotional too. In class a African American female student got emotional at the fact that we keep "downing African Americans". Bringing up the topic of white privilege is just like a broken record constantly repeating how unequal African Americans are to whites. Even though white privilege is very real, it is something that many African American people have already witnessed and seen first-hand. So why shove it into their faces again at school? This shows that many African American people are tired of hearing issues like this. This instance of the African American student getting emotional is important because the lesson of white privilege is making African American students feel like they can never escape the discussion of being seen as "less."

Not surprisingly, students at Stonebridge High School, who had predominantly referenced evidence related to personal experience in their two days of discussion, also overwhelmingly used the same form of support for their claims in writing. In fact, at the end of the second day's discussion, when the teacher mentioned students' needing supporting evidence when they wrote their letters to the Hope School Board, one student directly asked if supporting evidence could include personal examples. In response, Ms. Widerhaken assured: "Absolutely, you can. And you came up with some good stuff." Thus, student letters referred not only to examples from class discussion but also to new personal examples. One student, who identified as mixed race [Latinx and white] and opposed the teaching of the White Privilege curriculum, related a very long example of feeling excluded in a friend group due to her "mixed" heritage. Concluding her example, the student wrote:

> Teaching a white privilege class can cause students to feel guilty and hurt about the color of their skin (which they have no control of whatsoever) the same way that I felt when I was stereotyped for being full white. Someone else might say that teaching students about white privilege is not going to impact students in a negative way. It's not going to make students feel guilty for the color of their skin. But they need to realize that it impacts students way more than they think. Learning about white privilege can cause students to feel angry, sad, guilty, jealous, hurt and even depressed because it can either make (some) non-white students wish that they were born white, or it can make (some) white students dread the skin color that they were born with.

During the two class discussions, Stonebridge students rehearsed responding to positions opposing theirs. One example came during the second day of discussion:

> I believe that they should teach it [white privilege curriculum] because some people say that it will make the white students feel guilty. But it will only make them feel guilty only if they are doing such things. This would actually make them aware of . . . because not a lot of them are actually aware in such a white community. They are not aware of what they can get away with. So it would make them aware and it would probably help a future where everyone is treated more equal than they are now.

Although this speaker does not cite other commentary directly, she shows an awareness of an opposing view (i.e., those who worry that some students might feel guilty) that she feels a responsibility to address.

Later, one student, advocating the teaching of the White Privilege unit in writing to the Hope Board, developed an extended real-world example citing Dylann Roof, who had been arrested for killing nine members of a Bible study group in Charleston, South Carolina. This student argued that both blatant and subliminal racism stemmed from ignorance. In writing to counter arguments that the teaching about white privilege would only inflame racial tensions, the student wrote:

> Someone who disagrees with me might say that teaching white privilege will create tension between races but teaching and showing students the error of society's ways will bring them closer together instead of driving them apart which is the problem that white privilege causes so teaching it could end it and racism.

In referencing learning and awareness as an antidote to society's current state, the writer mirrors thoughts already raised in discussion. Hearing these ideas either introduced or reinforced points that the writer later transformed into support for his position.

In addition to citing personal examples, students also referred to articles they had read in their earlier research or heard referenced in discussions. Using a secondary source to buttress his opinion, one student advocating for teaching white privilege referred to the *New York Times* article "When Whites Just Don't Get It, Part 6" and quoted a study in which "a black applicant with a clean criminal record did no better than a white applicant who was said to have just been released from 18 months in prison." Further quoting from the article that the majority of whites believe that whites and blacks receive equal job opportunities, the student concluded, "If we teach the curriculum of white privilege, people may not think something like this because they will be educated on this topic." A second student, from another school but also supporting the teaching of the white privilege curriculum, cited another article from the research base: "An article about a high school in Wisconsin stated that 'a person who may benefit from white privilege is not necessarily racist or prejudiced and may be unaware of having any privileges reserved only for whites.' White students may not recognize they are benefiting from white privilege but when white and non-white students realize it they can show others how crucial white privilege truly is."

These examples illustrate the close connection between oral and written discourse. As students grappled together in discussions about a tough issue, they practiced procedures that served them as writers—summarizing, citing and interpreting evidence, and acknowledging and evaluating opposition. While we understand that writing supports students' thinking about complex issues (cf., Applebee & Langer, 2013), we also see how the discussion that precedes writing helps students to think about the substantive matters about which they are writing.

Extending the Inquiry: The Teaching about White Privilege Case

In some cases, the discussions that we observed were either the *gateways* into a multiweek line of inquiry or were the *culmination of inquiry* and supported the *synthesis* of texts and previous discussions. Ms. Zorba was able to incorporate the Teaching about White Privilege case into her students' extended inquiry of the seminal guiding question, "What do we do with difference?" This extended inquiry had students reading nonfiction and fiction, a graphic novel, and a Shakespearean play as they explored aspects of this question. As a first step, Ms. Zorba introduced her students to the protocols and language from Courageous Conversations about Race, work developed by the Pacific Education Group founded by Glenn E. Singleton. Courageous Conversations strategies provide the means by which classrooms can ensure safe and authentic dialogue among racially diverse students. These protocols gave students an elemental vocabulary that they practiced while discussing Jamal Joseph's autobiographical *Panther Baby*. During the reading of Yang's *American Born Chinese*, students explored the key question of "what do we do with a difference?" more directly by examining these questions:

- How do the tensions between the dominant and nondominant cultures shape the story?
- How does the story of the Monkey King address the guiding question?

In shaping the extended inquiry up to this point, Ms. Zorba used a compelling and very accessible nonfiction story as her students practiced the vocabulary of Courageous Conversations (e.g., dominant and nondominant culture) that would inform discussion in a later work of fiction that was more complex in its ideas while still accessible to her students in the graphic novel format. It was at this point that Ms. Zorba introduced the Teaching about White Privilege case to her students.

Ms. Zorba valued the role-playing segment of the case study for allowing her students to hear various perspectives on the issue in a nonthreatening way. In fact, one student, who wrote in favor of teaching the white privilege curriculum, chose to write in the persona of her assigned role-play character for her letter to the Hope Board of Education. In later conversation, Ms. Zorba identified this student as rather quiet, someone who rarely talked in class but had lots to say in writing. In her letter, the student made her case for teaching the white privilege curriculum with examples and addressed an argument of the opposition that she had heard in discussion. In her third paragraph, the student presents a convincing rationale for the extended inquiry her class had explored thus far as she cites the texts that she and classmates read and their connection to white privilege. Her argument reflects the synthesis of learning that had taken place with extended inquiry while presenting a convincing rationale for the extended inquiry approach.

Sample Student Letter to School Board

Dear Hope Board of Education,

I completely understand the frustration you may come across about this subject. Some people believe that if you just ignore this topic [white privilege], then it will go away. However, I strongly believe that as a social studies teacher at this school, the curriculum of white privilege is extremely valid and important to teach.

Last year, I decided to lightly touch upon the subject because I felt that it corresponded to the events that are going on in our world today. The students seemed to understand the concept of white privilege, but I got a bunch of e-mails and concerned parents. They told me that in teaching the concept of white privilege that it promotes racism, white guilt, and unnecessary tension among students. As a teacher I completely understand that I need to take student and parent's concerns into consideration. However, as a social studies teacher I need to make sure my students are getting a proper education. Personally, I'm not the type of person to sugar coat a real issue for the sake of feelings. I used to; but what I've learned as a social studies teacher is that history repeats itself if it's not addressed and acted upon.

I know that in their [referring to Hope students] English classes they are reading "Panther Baby" and "American Born Chinese." Two great books that touch upon non-fiction of what the world used to be like and realistic fiction of what discrimination is the most common nowadays. If those books are allowed to be read, it should be just as important to learn the concept you're reading about or else there is absolutely no point in reading something if you can't teach why something like that happened and why many things similar to that still go on.

Millikan students need this curriculum especially because they're not exposed to diversity, therefore when they go to college and the real world, they need to learn about other cultures, ethnicities, and issues as part of the white privilege curriculum. Millikan High School is made up of 65% Caucasian, 10% African American, 10% Latino, 10% Asian, and 5% mixed. These students lack the diversity that will hit them like a truck once they graduate. A lot of parents argue by saying that this topic is bringing up a lot of tension and that is understandable to see how that is upsetting to many parents, but as a teacher who is fighting for the teaching of this concept, I plan to keep an extremely peaceful, safe environment where students can respectfully debate their opinions with one another, but white privilege will still be taught as it is because if I ignore this real life issue, I'm lying to my students and depriving them of education that is extremely important to learn about. As a concerned teacher, white privilege will be taught in my class because it is too real to ignore. I can't look a student straight in the eyes and say "White privilege is not real," because it truly is. There's evidence to support it—just watch the news for 10 minutes and you'll see it. Until we recognize this issue and fight to end it, white privilege won't go away. Students deserve to know the sad truth.

Thank you,
Nina

Another of Ms. Zorba's students, a student reading at the seventh-grade level who also advocated the teaching of a white privilege unit in her letter to the Hope School Board, used a specific incident from her reading of *American Born Chinese* to illustrate and give support to her opinion. Ms. Zorba identified this student's writing as her best of the year. The writer's use of an elaborated example from *American Born Chinese* again illustrates the connections students are making as they explore concepts within an extended inquiry.

Student Letter Excerpt

In the book "American Born Chinese" on page 30-31 Jin Wang moved to a new neighborhood and the teacher introduces him to the class [saying], "he and his family recently moved to our neighborhood all the way from China!" [to which Jin responds,] "San Francisco" [whereupon the teacher self-corrects], "San Francisco!" (P. 30-31). She is white and so is the whole class besides Jin Wang so she mistakes him being from China just because he was Chinese. She thought he had moved from there, but he has lived in America his whole life. This is an example of racism and white privilege. If he was a new student that was white, she wouldn't have thought he came from Europe and said that. This is why places like Millikan High School need to teach the topic of white privilege so that things like this don't happen only to non-dominant groups in America. If we teach the curriculum of white privilege, things like this may not happen as much because people are aware of it.

Following their work with the Teaching about White Privilege case, Ms. Zorba's students read *Othello* as the culminating text of their extended inquiry. At this point, students were prepared to examine how the play's characters understood and manipulated race and gender differences in their reading of this more challenging text since they had already practiced their analysis of these key concepts with the earlier texts.

Extending the Inquiry: The Robot Teacher Case

In using the Robot Teacher case Ms. Torino also developed an extended line of inquiry with her students. She planned to use the case as a gateway activity for a unit of study on the relationship between technology and human interaction where her students would read Ray Bradbury's "The Veldt" and E. M. Forster's "The Machine Stops." However, an unplanned teacher absence falling between the students' role-playing discussion day and the students' discussion of the topic from their own perspectives prompted the students' reading of "The Veldt" in class during the interim day. Although unplanned, this arrangement demonstrates students' making connections between the story and the simulated case, as evidenced by this student's comment on the second day of class discussion: "I feel like once we decide to be taught by robots, we're going to be ruled by technology more than we are now. It goes back to what we were reading yesterday with 'The Veldt' and everything. They [characters in the story] were overtaken by all this new technology and it was taking over their lives. I feel like once we let technology raise the new generation, it will become something a little different."

After her students wrote their letters to the school board, Ms. Torino continued her originally intended sequence, spending more time discussing "The Veldt" and reading and discussing "The Machine Stops" with her students. Ms. Torino noted that students built upon the synergy created by the extended inquiry and "directly referenced the [Robot Teacher] case as a way to contextualize their points and draw parallels between the simulated experience and the discussion of the stories." Making the point that technology often falls short of its intended goal of nurturing and enhancing human interaction, one student connected "the robot teacher's limitations in making students more empathetic with the nursery's effect in making the children less obedient and more spoiled in 'The Veldt'," according to Ms. Torino.

Ms. Torino likened the short stories to "test cases that reaffirmed conclusions and deepened understandings drawn from the discussions about the limitations of the robot teacher." In support of this, Ms. Torino cited students who noted that technology created an irrevocable and malicious schism between parents and children in "The Veldt." However, challenging the simplicity of blaming lost communication solely on technology, another student in discussing "The Machine Stops" noted that technology may have initially hindered but ultimately enhanced human interaction. Thus, according to Ms. Torino, her students also modified and qualified initial observations through further observation and discussion of the topic in literature.

Some Other Possibilities for Extended Inquiry Discussions

If the discussion regarding the Teaching about White Privilege case is used as a gateway activity or as an activity within a larger unit of inquiry examining key concepts and questions such as Ms. Zorba's unit on Difference [What do we do with a difference?] or one on Social Justice [What does social justice look like?] or Identity [How do I define who I am? Why is it important to be aware of my identity?], of which white privilege is a part, teachers may choose from a wide variety of literature for student exploration. Short stories, poems, novels, essays, memoir, and film might include, but are certainly not limited to, the suggestions we offer in the sidebar list.

As a consequence of exploring the Teaching about White Privilege case, teachers and students may raise instances of white privilege in their later discussions of texts. However, the following activities suggest some ways of specifically exploring the concept with three different and rich texts from the list: *American Born Chinese* by Gene Luen Yang, *Citizen: An American Lyric* by Claudia Rankine, and *The Bluest Eye* by Toni Morrison. With some modification, these activities might easily be used with other texts as well.

Possible Texts for Exploration with the Teaching about White Privilege Case

Alexie, Sherman, *The Absolutely True Diary of a Part-Time Indian*
Baldwin, James, *Notes of a Native Son*
Beshir, Sumaiya, *Everyday Struggles: The Stories of Muslim Teens*
Cisneros, Sandra, *The House on Mango Street*
Cisneros, Sandra, "*The House on Mango Street*'s Tenth Birthday" in *A House of My Own: Stories of My Life*
Coates, Ta-Nehisi, *Between the World and Me*
Coates, Ta-Nehisi, "The Case for Reparations" in *The Atlantic*
Hilton, Marilyn, *Full Cicada Moon*
Hughes, Langston, "Theme for English B"
Irving, Debby, *Waking Up White*
Jefferson, Margot, *Negroland: A Memoir*
Kathari, Gaeta "Where Are You From?" in *Under Western Eyes*
Martinez, Victor *A Parrot in the Oven: Mi Vida*
Mora, Pat, "Le Migra" and "Legal Alien"
Morrison, Toni, *The Bluest Eye*
Rankine, Claudia, *Citizen: An American Lyric*
Shakespeare, William, *Othello*
Singer, Marilyn, *Face Relations: 11 Stories about Seeing beyond Color*
Steele, Claude, *Whistling Vivaldi*
Tan, Amy, "Mother Tongue" widely anthologized
Vargas, Jose Antonio, *White People*, an MTV documentary
Walker, Alice, "Without Commercials"
Wilson, August, *Two Trains Running*
Wise, Tim, *White Like Me*
Wright, Richard, *Native Son*
Yang, Gene Luen, *American Born Chinese*

Activity Models Prompting Extended Inquiry with Literature

We suggest that if students are going to engage critically with a series of texts that explore substantive issues, a teacher can design instructional activities that involve learners in extensive dialogue. In "Emotion, Reason, and Argument: Teaching Persuasive Writing in Tense Times," Smagorinsky (2018) contends that schools "tend to deflect and discourage attention to emotional issues like racism, misogyny, and many sensitive issues raised in much of young adult literature" (p. 99). As a way of addressing these issues, Smagorinsky suggests posing three questions: What gut feeling is behind this point of view? What values motivate this point of view? Are these values learned or inborn?

For example, with text found on page 91 of *American Born Chinese*, we would ask students to study several frames carefully. These color frames show the dark-and-straight-haired Jin thinking of his dream girl Amelia, a blonde, talking with her lab partner, Greg, a curly-haired blond. Thinking about the differences between Greg and himself, Jin has an idea regarding how he might alter his appearance to more resemble Greg's in order to attract Amelia's attention. Breaking students into small groups, we would ask them to respond to the following questions:

1. What gut feeling is behind Jin's point of view? How do you know?
2. What values motivate Jin's point of view? How do you know?
3. Are these values learned or inborn?

Reconvening as a whole class, we would ask students to share their answers, continuing to discuss and support their views with evidence from the text. Of course, the discussion may well end with several ideas as long as they are supported by the text and extend to connections with white privilege. Using other frames and other characters, teachers may use Smagorinsky's questions multiple times within a text as well as use them with other types of reading such as essays and editorials to prompt discussion and explore authorial intent. Within the Teaching about White Privilege case study, it might also be useful for students assuming the various roles within the role-play portion to ask these three questions with reference to the persona they are assuming and representing.

Another activity that can be adapted to any number of texts exploring the concept of white privilege is shown in Figure 6.1. We have used activities such as this with a variety of texts and genres to great effect (cf. Wilhelm, 2016). In the midst of reading, teachers ask students to inhabit a character as a passage

Figure 6.1. Articulating subtexts.

Directions: For each segment of text below, write down what the two speakers are thinking as actions are taken and words are spoken in this segment.

Speaker 1	Text	Speaker 2

of dialogue or description is read aloud and to respond to questions such as "What are you thinking?" and "What are you feeling?" in character. An activity such as this may be done orally or in writing first with an opportunity to discuss later in a variety of ways. For example, we might first present and read the vignette found on page 44 of Rankine's *Citizen: An American Lyric,* in which an African American employee and a manager meet face to face after speaking on the phone. Presenting each segment of the vignette's text within a separate box, we would ask students, either individually or in pairs, to complete thought bubbles for each dialogue participant. Thus, the first row in Figure 6.1 would include the following text: "At the end of a brief phone conversation, you tell the manager you are speaking with that you will come by his office to sign the form. When you arrive and announce yourself, he blurts out, I didn't know you were black!" (p. 44). Students will have a variety of responses for what Speaker 1—in this case, "You / the speaker"—might be thinking upon hearing the manager's comment: possibly "Really, race is the first thing you think about?" or "How are Black people supposed to sound?" or "I came to sign a form. Race is irrelevant" or "I am who I am. Who are you?" Students will also have a variety of possible thought responses for Speaker 2—in this case, "the manager"—possibly including "That just popped out" or "Probably not PC" or "You didn't sound Black on the phone." Students should share and discuss their responses with the entire class as each row of text is considered or upon completion of the entire exchange.

We can offer as a third example that we have used surveys or questionnaires in the past not only to solicit student readers' initial reactions and feelings on a topic but also to allow students to view a topic from a character's perspective once they have read a text (Johannessen, Kahn, & Walter, 2009). The questions in the Figure 6.2 activity have been adapted or excerpted from and inspired by those presented in "The Invisible Backpack" (McIntosh, 1989) and may be used with further adaptation or addition with any number of characters and texts.

Synergy Before, During, and After

Curricular needs, student interest, even unplanned absence may shape the ways in which instruction is delivered, but the synergy developed through extended inquiry among various texts and activities, especially those related to high interest topics, is not only evident within our study but also important to provide for our students. In the examples of the teachers we profile in this book, we have seen that discussions are not isolated events, but are part of a sequence—either to prepare for writing elaborated compositions, to introduce an extended line of

Figure 6.2. What do you think?

Directions: Read all of the questions below and respond in the first column as yourself by circling your yes or no response. Be prepared to support your responses as "Picola" with specific reference to *The Bluest Eye*.

	You	Picola
1. If I or my family or a close friend needs to move, I can be pretty sure of renting or purchasing housing in an area I can afford and in which I would want to live.	Yes. No.	Yes. No.
2. I can be pretty sure that my neighbors in such a location will be pleasant or neutral to me, my family, and friends.	Yes. No.	Yes. No.
3. If my day, week, or year is going badly, I need not ask of each negative experience or situation whether it has racial overtones.	Yes. No.	Yes. No.
4. I can go home from most activities I regularly engage in [e.g. school, a store, or a classmate's home] feeling somewhat tied in, rather than isolated, out of place, outnumbered, unheard, held at a distance, or feared.	Yes. No.	Yes. No.

inquiry, or to synthesize the reading of a series of related texts. The discussions about consequential matters represented in contemporary cases were part of a sustained and connected conversation, with many variations and complications, but always with the goal of increased exploration and understanding.

7 What Teachers Need to Know about Discussion

Each of us has had a long career in teaching English in high schools, including public and private, urban and suburban, large and small, predominantly white middle class and poor and highly diverse, alternative and conventional. We have tried to make discussion the core element of our instruction, with mixed success during our early years of teaching, with greater confidence and effect across years of practice. As we have now turned to preparing prospective teachers to cultivate a dialogic classroom, we have studied the impact that authentic discussions have on literacy learning and have attempted to identify the features of instruction that promote dialogue. We have endeavored to reflect candidly on our own practices, both as we recall ourselves as high school teachers and as we continue to work in classrooms at the university and in public schools. We have to admit that we often fall short of our idealized vision of a dialogic classroom, but we know how powerful discussion can be for literacy learning and how satisfying extended discussions can be for adolescents who need to connect with peers, grapple with ideas and problems, and construct their own sense of meaning and understanding.

We understand how uncommon authentic discussion is in most classrooms, and we appreciate from our own experience and from our efforts to prepare teachers for the classroom that it is difficult for many teachers to immerse themselves and their students in a genuine line of inquiry and to engage in discussions with flexibility and responsiveness to learners' needs and interests. At the same time, we see great promise in being able to engage adolescents frequently in extensive discussions about issues that the students see as consequential, even when those discussions seem like they would be awkward or potentially volatile.

When we reflect on the teachers and students whom we profile in the earlier chapters of this book, we confirm for ourselves that extensive classroom discussion need not be reserved for a privileged student population in elite schools. When Tom was in his early years of teaching, he taught in an alternative school where he relied on discussion as the primary mode of instruction. The students in Tom's classes had dropped out of school and were reentering in an "alternative environment." Perhaps Tom didn't know any better and neglected more controlled possibilities for English instruction, but the discussions in his classes seemed to function constructively and served as preparation for writing and as a means for reflecting on the literature the classes read together. Although we can be fooled by general impressions, Tom recalls that students generally enjoyed the opportunities to talk to each other as an essential part of their learning in an English class. The frequent opportunities to interact with peers seemed to satisfy a need among the students in an alternative school, and we have seen similar signs of satisfaction among students in a variety of classrooms.

In Chapter 3, we conjecture about the factors that encourage students to participate in and sustain discussions about consequential problems. Certainly, several factors have an effect: who the learners are, what they choose to discuss, how a group proceeds in discussing, and what a teacher does to support inquiry and civil discourse and to connect discussions as part of an extended effort at examining issues and understanding concepts. We understand that the kind of extensive discussions that we have observed do not depend on exceptional students and distinctively gifted teachers, although we judge that the students we observed were bright and talented and the teachers distinguished. But authentic discussions do not have to depend on optimum circumstances and rare teachers. The factor over which teachers have the greatest control is what they do themselves.

As we report earlier in the book, in four different schools (small town, suburban, and urban environments), we observed discussions about the same controversial problem. The students in the urban classroom were almost all African American; the suburban schools were highly diverse—culturally, linguistically, and economically. In the classrooms, across a sequence of lessons and across four schools, students consistently did more than 50 percent of the talking, in conversations that were purposeful and focused on the problem at hand. We learned from the teachers and students we observed that sustained discussion about consequential problems is possible almost anywhere. But we also learned that for the discussions to engage learners and sustain the thinking about consequential and complex problems, the teacher needed to do much to prepare and needed to command some core pedagogical moves. In the balance of this chapter, we summarize that preparation and the core actions to promote, sustain, and connect discussion.

Fostering genuine inquiry and authentic discussion is a complicated endeavor, and to summarize what teachers might do to foster inquiry and sustain the related discussions might almost trivialize the processes that teachers follow. Nevertheless, we will offer a broad outline here and trust that teachers can refine practice through their own attempts and reflections.

Planning and Inviting Discussions

As a first consideration, a teacher should recognize that learners are not going to contribute willingly to discussions if they fear they will be ridiculed or disrespected, or if they are convinced that they are not competent at the skills that the teacher and classmates appear to value. The implication, then, is that teachers need to cultivate safe classroom environments that will allow peers to talk to each other freely, candidly, and respectfully, and will recognize learners for what they know, not what they don't know yet. The teachers we have observed have all created supportive learning environments, although each has proceeded in a different way. We know of no formula for establishing a safe and supportive learning environment, but we recognize some common efforts among the teachers we observed.

First, the teachers we observed knew their students well. The teachers came to know the students from talking to them and from reading their writing. We took the formal step of surveying students about the contemporary issues that were critical to them. Whether or not a teacher relies on a survey, the daily interchanges with students, especially as part of talking about literature and film, reveal what concerns students and what excites their passions. The idea that a teacher would care enough to inquire about what learners value is likely to seem to the students to be a welcome distinction.

Getting to know who your students are—what interests them, what worries them, what excites them, what irritates them, etc.—is part of developing a positive rapport. A rapport is different from a friendship: It is a positive relationship built on respect and empathy. Ms. Widerhaken at the urban Stonebridge High School noted explicitly that she thought of the class as a family. She greeted everyone warmly and reacted sympathetically when someone was distressed and demonstrably happy when she learned of someone's accomplishment. But other teachers operated respectfully by listening attentively and responding politely. A combination of relatively simple moves and responses added up to a feeling of comfort, if not perfect harmony.

In some instances, a class might engage together in establishing the norms for interaction. The organizational leaders at Google spent millions of dollars in studying what features distinguish the most productive working groups. They examined many factors: whether or not group members were introverts or extroverts, whether people preferred to meet only during working hours, whether or not there was a gender balance in the group, and so on. There was no clear pattern, except that the most functional groups were those who established some rules for how they were going to work together and then stuck to those rules. Similarly, students in a class, whether in small groups or operating as a whole, can say what they expect from their classmates and how they prefer to work with others. These overtly expressed rules can guide interactions and remain the standard to which discussion participants can refer in assessing their own behavior and in talking about how communication could improve.

Ultimately the teacher serves as the model and the arbitrator. Among the teachers we observed, we have seen instances when a teacher rephrased a student's response to soften the tone, and a teacher redirected behavior that moved away from the purpose for the discussion or that bordered on impoliteness. At the same time, we would hate to see a teacher try to suppress a student because the student's strongly held belief seemed to the teacher to be misguided. We urge teachers to trust in an inquiry process, knowing that for every student who seems to be looking at a problem illogically, there will be another student who poses the appropriate question or offers a rebuttal. We would not like to see the teacher descend into a one-on-one debate with a learner, especially when the issues at the heart of the discussion have a political dimension. If the students are indeed engaged in inquiry, the teacher will have to check herself for subtle violations of the spirit and processes of inquiry. In our experiences as supervisors of classroom teachers, we have witnessed at least one teacher who asked tough follow-up questions to the students with whom he clearly disagreed and offered only paraphrases of the responses of students with whom he agreed. It is certainly important to ask the questions that will prompt students to develop ideas fully and logically, but the line of questioning should not become a teacher's attempt to indoctrinate learners into his own point of view, even when it seems clearly reasonable and righteous to the teacher. Students recognize in an instant when a teacher appears to respond in ways that seem to be unfair; and the perception of unfairness can do much to rupture rapport.

Learning How to Facilitate Discussions

While having a conversation seems intuitive, facilitating an instructional conversation requires some developed skills. We do not know how much instruction the teachers featured in this book have had to prepare them to be able to plan and facilitate discussions in their classrooms. In Chapters 4 and 5, you see evidence of the teachers at work in prompting discussions and fostering inquiry, but you see only glimpses of them at work with their students. They had to do much to plan for the discussions: selecting the focus for discussions that would connect with a broader line of inquiry, framing a problem that matters to the learners, allowing time for students to prepare to enter into conversation,

Discussion Pathways to Literacy Learning: Learning How to Facilitate Discussions

Planning and Inviting Discussions

- Develop rapport with and construct a safe space for students to talk to each other about issues of consequence.
- Learn about the learners to discover their perceptions about problems and questions that resonate with them.
- Trust in an authentic inquiry process to bring facts to the surface, foster deep understandings, and refine processes.

Practicing in the Moment

- Teach students how to function in a dialogic classroom.
- Keep goals in mind to sequence experiences and guide actions from moment to moment.
- Slow down processes of inquiry and dialogue to honor understandings and not to speed through coverage.
- Assess learners' contributions carefully in order to judge the focus, pace, extent of participation, and impact.
- Promote genuine inquiry rather than indoctrination.
- Extend discussions through various means beyond the classroom.
- Connect the sequence of discussions as part of a coherent program of inquiry.
- Sequence inquiry and discussion as an expanding and deepening effort toward understanding and refined communication.
- Connect discussions to compelling texts and elaborated writing.

Reflecting on Practice

- Reflect candidly on how discussions supported instructional goals and prepare students for subsequent learning.
- Tally the participation—the number of participants, the dominant participants, and the noncontributors.
- Track the pattern and direction of participation.
- Look closely at what is being said during discussion, with an eye toward the intellectual moves that you assume discussion supports.

initiating discussion with questions that invited dialogue (or making a "dialogic bid," as Nystrand [1997] says), organizing the forums for discussion, and assessing evidence of the intellectual moves that discussion should encourage.

We insist that teachers have to learn how to facilitate authentic discussions. Facilitating discussions about consequential problems with groups of adolescents is not an intuitive endeavor. Nystrand (1997) compares the process to building a fire: starting with something to ignite conversation, gradually adding to the development through questions and invitations to participants, and building to significant effects as many thinkers join in the conversation. We have seen time and again when a teacher does not capitalize on a dialogic moment, by failing to ask an appropriate follow-up question, by neglecting to invite other students to respond, or by dominating the conversation. In these instances, potentially rich dialogic discourse descends into recitation and affirmation of the teacher's point of view. Teachers can easily fool themselves into thinking a class meeting was rich with discussion. As we have noted earlier, Hillocks (1999) reports a case in which a teacher expressed satisfaction about the class "discussion," when actually only one student spoke, and that was to apologize for being tardy.

As with the development of any skill, for a teacher to become skillful at facilitating discussions, she will have to practice, collect data on the result of her attempts, and assess honestly the effect of her efforts. A good place to start is with a current news story, a survey, a scenario, a problem case, or a story or poem that the teacher can admit to understanding only slightly. In other words, a good place to start is where a teacher has genuine doubts—perhaps about defining a concept, applying a standard, deciding a course of action, evaluating a character's behavior, or interpreting a text. As we suggest in Chapter 5, there are many simple means that a teacher can rely on to assess the effect of instruction—tallying participation, tracking the direction and extent of participation, recording discussions and transcribing portions, etc. While we commend the teachers featured in Chapter 3 for achieving the noteworthy distinction of having students account for more than 50 percent of the talking during the discussions about teaching the concept of white privilege, we know that the teachers could look at the discussion transcripts and see many places where they could have asked other questions or encouraged students to say more.

A friend of ours is both an engineer and a business manager. He flies all over the world on business, following a grueling pace and venturing into unfamiliar territory. We recall how we have returned exhausted from the NCTE Annual Convention after we stayed in a town only a few states away for a mere three days. We can't imagine venturing into places we deem exotic and foreign unless we are thoroughly prepared and assured of safety and comfort. But our friend is a seasoned traveler and an accomplished engineer. He travels with an attitude that once he arrives somewhere and runs into difficulty, he can always engineer his way out of the problem. He makes plans on the fly and adjusts those plans in response to the conditions he discovers. In some ways, a teacher who immerses herself and her class in extensive authentic discussions will be venturing into uncharted territory and must respond to the conditions she discovers. This is both scary and exhilarating. It is the exhilaration that comes with discovery and learning. You can become the confident engineer in the territory of open dialogue about consequential problems if you are experienced in practice and problem-solving. So, we encourage teachers to learn the rudiments of facilitating discussion, and practice, practice, practice.

Deciding and Problem-Solving in the Moment

A provocative question or an intriguing problem can inspire students to contribute much to discussions. But the facilitation of sustained and connected authentic discussions requires more than discovering the right problem or mastering "questioning techniques." Our close look at the practices of teachers who have engaged students in a series of linked conversations that were part of ongoing inquiry reveals that teachers have made significant decisions in the moment to keep discussion authentic and to foster habits of thinking.

First, we acknowledge that any discussion in a classroom is probably better than no discussion at all; but we want teachers to proceed with purpose. If "discussion" is really recitation, then the teacher's purpose is to hear the accurate reporting of the answers that the teacher has in mind. This might have a place if the teacher is assessing the extent to which students have read and understood a text. If this is the case, the teacher will want to ask the right questions to prompt responses, or might on occasion have to reword questions if students seem confused. The teacher will know when the discussion has played out when she has heard the responses she hopes to hear, or when he recognizes that the students are not able to respond, because they have not read or they have not understood. If, however, a teacher has other purposes in mind, she will have to assess and adjust in the moment. In principle, the teacher's instructional goals direct the sequence of experiences and guide actions from moment to moment. If, as in the examples of the teachers profiled in this book, the teacher hopes that the students develop the knowledge and skills necessary to produce an elaborated written response to a complex policy question, she will prompt students to exhibit that knowledge and those skills. If we take as an example the discussion about the Teaching about White Privilege case, we have observed teachers do the following:

- Ask students to *summarize* what the core problem is
- Invite students to *argue in support of a position* about the problem
- Prompt students to *support claims*
- Press students to *interpret data* offered as evidence
- Require students to *paraphrase an opposing point of view* in order to situate an argument
- Ask students to *compare two or more points of view* to reveal which one offers more benefits and fewer disadvantages.

As the conversation plays out dynamically and organically, the teacher listens for evidence that students can do in discussion all that an elaborated argument requires: *summarize, support, interpret, analyze,* and *synthesize*. How a teacher follows up with questions and how a teacher highlights and labels responses all depend on the projected learning outcomes. The following exchange reveals a teacher's decision making in the moment.

WESTON: Yeah. Why are you all up in arms about the whole topic? Nobody knows.

MS. BREZEL: Weston was not here yesterday for the beginning of this. Can someone summarize? Yes, Alicia, go for it. Thank you.

ALICIA: It looks like perks and advantages that white people are supposed to get or whatever just because they are white. So like if students end up being in the school office and thinking the flesh color Band-Aid is supposed to look like the natural color for them. That is part of being a white. Band-Aid as "natural" is a symptom [class laughing]. If I stay in a hotel, the complimentary shampoo works on your hair but it doesn't work on my hair. That is one part. They make it work for white people. I don't even know how I would think about that, but again . . .

MS. BREZEL: What about shopping?

ALICIA: You are shopping, and they do follow me because I am black but they don't follow you because you are white. If a group of white kids on the street . . .

JAMES: You are not going to get away with stealing or something, but for a group of white kids on the corner, just talking, they go ahead, while I get pressured because black kids are supposed to be like this. If I get pulled over, I am more likely to get, "you are not allowed to speed anymore." I was taught to be aware of white privilege as a subject.

Here the teacher recognizes that a student cannot enter into the conversation unless he is aware of the problem that the class is discussing. Ms. Brezel asks for a summary and follows up by asking a student to elaborate about the concept that she describes. She invites a second speaker to add to the description of the complexity of the concept. As the facilitator for the discussion, Ms. Brezel does not appear to be looking for recitation or consensus, but prompts students to contribute for the sake of clarity.

Similarly, in Ms. Widerhaken's class at Stonebridge High School, the teacher does not affirm that anyone has the "correct" answer, but paraphrases to check for clarity and to encourage reactions from other students. When Ms. Widerhaken asks students questions, she is not challenging their position, but is revealing that she may have misunderstood and seeks to correct her misunderstanding. In the following exchange, you can get a graphic sense that Ms. Widerhaken is following the discussion closely, checking that she understands, attending to those waiting to respond, and calling on as many students as possible. She prompts students to elaborate, but she relies on classmates to challenge each other or to add nuances to the discussion of the problem.

KYLA: I am "just" a black person. I mean, I don't know about white people's any special rights. So I am not going know too much about it being a white, if you think about it.

ANDREA: I got something to say.

MS. WIDERHAKEN: Go ahead.

ANDREA: I feel that we should teach it because it can prepare you better for realism. In my opinion, I am just like whites who are always having it more easy. So like you never learn about it, you never realize it, it wouldn't be a surprise whatsoever.

MS. WIDERHAKEN: You are thinking as a Stonebridge High School student. Is that correct? I think this is what you are saying. Correct me, if I am wrong. I think you are thinking along the line that if you are growing up in a dominant minority community and you don't see the whites are treated differently, that could be a shock to your system when you leave that community and go in somewhere that is more predominantly white and you are not treated the same way? Is that what you are saying?

ANDREA: Yeah.

MS. WIDERHAKEN: If we're still looking at the curriculum including the white privilege at Millikan, we have to consider their ethnic makeup. What is the percentage of the school, 60 percent white?

KYLA: Like if a black child is trying to be into a program, and they get it, then they are all like, "Oh. They get in just because they are not white."

MS. WIDERHAKEN: OK.

THOMAS: All right. I don't think it really matters, if you think about it. I don't think it matters to teach it because whether you are teaching it or not, with the history book we have, they have already shown how glorious white people had been. They keep that. Christopher Columbus discovered North America. The white people can do more stuff like that. History books have already shown that white people are glorious. There is not much about black people in history books. So I mean, whether you are teaching it or not, it is in the history book already.

MS. WIDERHAKEN: Are you suggesting that is obvious? Is that what you mean?

THOMAS: Yeah.

JANETTE: Could I go ahead?

MS. WIDERHAKEN: Yeah. Go ahead.

JANETTE: I haven't really seen this because [inaudible] as an art student, I haven't learned a lot about black people. You know there were black people in history but it is always mainly about white people so to speak. Even now this year . . . [inaudible].

MS. WIDERHAKEN: Keep on it, then.

JANETTE: Me, as an African American student, has a Caucasian friend . . . it will be like problems with schools and art school teachers with white privilege. It basically makes it seem better to me. I mean, I probably wouldn't have a problem with it personally. But other black people probably would.

The two brief exchanges above reveal that students are discussing complicated concepts and perplexing issues. It is important that a teacher does not try to speed through the process. In many ways, dialogue and inquiry require the teacher to slow down. There is no point in moving forward to the next element in the curriculum if students are not demonstrating in discussion that they understand a complex idea and that they can exhibit the habits of thinking that are important for critical reading, elaborated writing, and mature decision making.

We were fortunate to be able to observe classes with teachers who taught the learners how to participate in authentic discussion. To paraphrase Benjamin Bloom, if you want students to do something (e.g., listen attentively and critically to others, represent opposing ideas fairly and accurately), you have to teach them how to do it. In many ways, Ms. Brezel and Ms. Widerhaken above model how to paraphrase, check for understanding, admit misunderstanding, invite further views, etc. What the teacher demonstrates in front of learners serves as a powerful model that students imitate to an extent when they join together in small groups as well as in whole class discussion.

Connecting Discussions as Part of Inquiry

As we discuss in Chapter 6, the teachers we have studied have connected discussions to other significant literacy learning—first by asking students for a written analysis of a case, and later by applying similar thinking to their critical reading of complex texts. We encourage teachers to think beyond a single discussion. While any authentic discussion is likely to have a positive effect on literacy learning, learners are likely to experience a greater impact on their writing and their reading of significant works of literature if they can engage frequently in discussions, especially those that build on each other in a connected line of inquiry (Applebee, 1996; Langer, 2001).

In the examples that we highlight throughout the book, the series of discussions build on each other. When students are tackling a complex contemporary problem, they first work in small groups to discuss what they read and to construct preliminary arguments. This preparation stage is necessary to allow students to engage productively in a simulated meeting that exposes everyone to a variety of ways of thinking about the problem. This meeting that showcases competing arguments and several options for responding to a problem is necessary for students to be ready for a discussion about their personal responses to critical issues. In a limited way, the simulated meeting serves the same purpose as a literature review for a thesis—a broad scan of information and perspectives to refine how to define the problem, evaluate possible solutions, and find a place for one's individual voice in the broad conversation. If we think backwards across a series of school days, the pattern is this: We can't have Thursday's discussion about the various options unless we have Wednesday's simulated meeting to showcase those options, and we can't showcase the options unless we have Tuesday's small group discussions to prepare participants to offer their analyses and arguments. As we have argued elsewhere (McCann, 2014; McCann, D'Angelo, Galas, & Greska, 2015), students learn to write by talking. As the examples in this book show, as students talk to each other about a substantive issue, they practice many essential procedures that, with the teacher's support, transfer to their written responses.

Beyond the immediate impact that the discussions have on students' writing, the discussions that we observed either served as a gateway into a line of inquiry into a complex concept or served as a means for synthesizing the reading and discussions across a thematic unit. In this context, the series of discussions about the prospect of robot teachers could raise questions about the importance of human relationships and the role that technology plays in our lives. The series of discussions about studying the concept of white privilege might extend into explorations about identity, equity, and justice. In these instances, the teacher is thinking strategically about how the discussions in a gateway activity might activate prior knowledge and equip students with critical questions that can guide their reading of several connected texts. The discussions then continue and build on each other as students explore complications and nuances. These connected discussions help students to refine their thinking and sharpen their communication about their judgments and discoveries.

Of course, discussions do not have to be limited to the classroom. Various online means allow students to share their thoughts and enter into conversations in a digital environment. In some instances, students who might have been hesitant to share their opinions in class are ready to react to a blog or to post to an online discussion. The same protocols and rules for civility apply in a digital environment that a teacher can monitor. Even with some teacher monitoring, students can discuss online in an environment that they think of as their space for sharing. These online discussions can serve as starting points for continuing discussions in the classroom.

Whether discussions occur in the classroom alone or both in the classroom and online, a teacher will want to monitor the conversations to judge how students remain focused, whether the pace is too slow or too fast, how many students are participating, how extensive are the contributions, how civil are the responses, and what evidence there is that students understand content and can practice the procedures for analysis, evaluation, and argument. Some intriguing questions and complex problems—like the concept of white privilege, the role of technology in our lives, the justice and efficacy of *predictive discipline* or *restorative justice*—are just too complicated to dispense with in a single class meeting. Inquiries into these concepts and problems have many dimensions and complications. As discussions progress and move into texts of various sorts, a teacher will make decisions about staying on course and whether or not a class has demonstrated sufficient understanding about one dimension of the problem to be able to move on to the next. Considered in this way, a series of connected discussions require monitoring and decision making, taking an organic form that is difficult to script.

Reflecting on Practice

We know that we have been as guilty as anyone of ending a class and thinking we had a great discussion, when in actuality we dominated the talk or we relied on a few eager students to carry the conversation. If discussion is going to enrich learners' experiences and enhance their literacy learning, then it must be authentic, involve many students, and emphasize the procedures that one can reasonably expect to transfer to writing elaborated compositions and reading complex texts critically.

We have observed teachers who have taken a variety of steps to check that the "discussion" was indeed *discussion*. A first step is to be mindful of who is responding, how many students are contributing, and how they are contributing. But it might *seem* that a lot of students from around the classroom are joining in the conversation when in actuality the usual few contributors talk most frequently. Not everyone has to contribute to every discussion, but it is good practice to be aware of the discourse patterns in the classroom. Occasionally a colleague might visit your classroom to chart the discussion through a simple tally of who contributed and how often each person contributed. A look at the tallies might prompt several questions for reflection: Do the same students tend to dominate the discussion? Where are the most frequent contributors located in the classroom? Are the most vocal contributors male or female? Who never contributes? Why is this the case?

We have also seen teachers solicit the aid of one student per class to track the classroom discourse. This might be through a process developed by George Hillocks. Whoever is tracking the discussion would rely on a simple seating chart and draw a line with an arrow from the speaker to whomever the comment is directed (see Figure 5.8). As the speaker continues, draw a hash mark across the line every three seconds. For every subsequent contribution, the observer again places a hash mark across the line that indicates the direction of the comment. In the end, the chart will offer a visual representation of the discussion: Who contributes, and how often? Who does not contribute, and why might this be the case? Do all of the lines and arrows point to the teacher? How can the conversation move away from the dominance of the teacher and move to an exchange from student to student?

We have known teachers who have recorded a class discussion and relied on voice recognition software to transcribe the exchanges. In this way, the whole class can look beyond how many learners participated and can examine closely what participants are saying: Are they supporting claims? Do they practice *uptake*? Do they fairly and accurately represent the contributions of their classmates? Do they evaluate logically the contributions of others? This kind of practice helps the learners to recognize and label the intellectual moves they are making during discussions, and helps the teacher to be aware of who is contributing, how many are contributing, and how they are contributing. In this way, when a teacher reflects on how great the discussion was during any particular class meeting, she will have some data with which to check her impression.

Final Thoughts

Our observations of teachers and students as they engaged in substantive discussions have given us hope. We see that teachers in various settings can engage students in sustained and connected discussions. We see that students can learn how to engage in civil and rational conversations that probe deeply into significant issues. We recognize that through involvement, in one way or another, in a series of related discussions, students learn procedures that support written expression and critical reading of complex texts. Most important, we find hope in the fact that diverse groups of students can discuss a controversial topic, especially one that touches on race-based discrimination, in a constructive and honest way. We witnessed emotional moments and strained episodes during the discussions we observed, but the discussions continued constructively, and students contended with challenges and disagreements in a way that never deteriorated into shouting, ridicule, or insult.

We see that in the classroom it is possible to discuss at length thorny problems that can seem potentially volatile. In fact, we judge that it is not only possible, but necessary. Just as we expect students to learn many other aspects of functioning as a member of a democratic society through their classroom experiences, we judge that students can learn how to grapple together about emotionally charged contentious issues—e.g., about diversity, identity, equity, and justice—by interacting with each other frequently in evaluating tough problems and seeking solutions. As Cindy O'Donnell-Allen (2011) describes, we fear that too often teachers avoid discussions about tough issues, worried about potential classroom conflict, parent complaints, or imagined community outcry. Such avoidance leaves teachers in search of tame themes and passive activities. In exercising such caution, when it is clear to us that teachers and students can learn how to have candid and constructive conversations about difficult topics, teachers deny students the opportunities to learn the essentially democratic tools of talking with others when problems are both contentious and complicated. In fact, we are not sure how students will ever learn how to talk with others, even those who vehemently oppose them, when they never have such opportunities in the classroom. They are certainly not going to learn from watching cable news programs or by witnessing how disputes are most often settled in school hallways, on playgrounds, and on street corners.

So, our final thought is to encourage teachers to move forward boldly, but not rashly. Following the examples of the teachers we have observed, other teachers can engage students in extensive discussions about difficult issues that students find engaging and consequential. But the bold teacher also has to plan carefully to foster a safe and supportive environment, organize the structures that shepherd students through an authentic inquiry process, and respond appropriately to encourage critical thinking and civil engagement.

Appendix A: Survey of Student Interest

What do you want to talk about? Perhaps you have thought from time to time that your classes put you in a position of discussing and reading about problems that don't particularly concern you. Your teacher is interested in discovering what problems capture your interest and would be the kind of topics that you might enjoy discussing with classmates. Consider each of the following brief stories and the debatable issues that the story suggests. Rate the stories according to the following scale:

4 = This story interests me, and I am eager to talk about it with my friends and classmates.

3 = This story holds some interest, and I wouldn't mind talking about it with my classmates.

2 = This story is only marginally interesting, and I could be encouraged to talk about it with classmates.

1 = This story doesn't interest me at all, and I would find it annoying to talk about it.

_____ **Stop all the fighting:** Some parents and other residents of the towns that support Upper Bascomb County High School would like to see the school change its mascot and the "spirit" song to be consistent with the school's declared campaign to discourage violence and promote tolerance and understanding. The mascot is the "Fighting Tar," a pugnacious sailor. Critics point out that the school's spirit song contains no less than thirteen instances of the word *fight* or its variants. While the anti-violence critics want to replace the song and the mascot, traditionalists claim that the song and mascot do not promote violence and should be preserved as part of the rich tradition of the school in a community that has long ties with the sea and sailing.

Go, go, Upper Bascomb County High,
Fight for the Tars, fight, fight fight!
We are the fighting Tars, as you know:
Just start a fight and watch us go.
So, here's to the Tars, the fighters true,
They'll fight, fight, fight, for me and you.
Let's raise the colors to the heights
And go ol' Tars, let's fight, fight, fight!

_____ **It's a brave new classroom:** There already are robot bartenders and driverless cars, so it should come as no surprise that the Huxley Corporation has produced a robot teacher. The current model is called Alpha Master. While quite advanced compared to earlier attempts, the Alpha Master models are still in a developmental stage and are quite expensive. The Foundation for Liberty and Prosperity has agreed to fund the piloting of the use of five robot teachers at Floodrock High School. If the school board agrees, in the coming school year, the five Alpha Masters will teach US history, beginning Chinese, and three different math classes. The manufacturer claims that the robot teachers never tire, lose patience, get distracted, or disseminate inaccuracies. They monitor and record students' behavior constantly, attend assiduously to provisions for students' special needs, and communicate with parents quickly and frequently. Some traditionalists and the local teachers' union resist this move and fear that instruction will become depersonalized and insensitive. If the experiment is successful, it could mean the long-term replacement of teachers with robots. In fact, many teachers fear that the agenda of the Huxley Corporation is to replace most teachers in the country with robots.

_____ **Wazzup!** A social media app called "Wazzup!" allows contributors within a limited range (e.g., within twenty miles of a college campus) to post messages on a continuous feed. Students on college campuses use the app to share where parties are happening, where drugs are available, and how they got wasted recently. Parents of high school seniors have tapped into this feed to gain insight into the social environment of the colleges where their sons or daughters have applied for admission. Many students complain that the parents have misrepresented themselves as students and have intruded into the private world of the life on the college campus. For their part, college and university professors have been appalled by what they have seen on "Wazzup!" They fret that parents and potential students will get the wrong idea about their institutions by depending on the incoherent postings by a relative few drug-addled and alcohol-soaked undergraduates. Some more proactive professors have started to post their own messages about upcoming lectures, art exhibits, concerts, plays, poetry readings, and other elements of the cultural and intellectual life of the campus. These professors hope that their counternarrative will leave a more positive impression on parents. Many high school seniors would like to see their parents and the college professors remove themselves from the "Wazzup!" exchanges, noting that their intrusions are both dishonest and inappropriate.

_____ **Make the Boys Cry:** Two facts distinguish the youth hockey team known as the Crashers: They are undefeated, and they are all girls in a male-dominated league. For many of the boys, it has been humiliating to lose, and lose convincingly, to an all-girls team. But one can hardly constrain the girls in any way just because they are highly skilled players, even if some feelings are hurt, as they are in any sport. Nevertheless, some opposing players, their parents, and coaches have complained on two fronts: The coach for the Crashers is Ned Chuzzle, a former professional hockey player who brings a world of experience and hockey knowledge into his training and coaching regimen. No other team has a comparable coach. The coach closes practice to parents, so no one knows how he pushes the girls to extract the level of performance that no other team sees. Some opponents have also complained that the girls have subtly taunted the boys after the Crashers have taken the lead in a game or executed a particularly athletic play. The more sensitive boys have noted that it is the taunting, apparently encouraged by Coach Chuzzle, and not the losing that has goaded them into crying. The governing board of the league now wonders if they should rein in Coach Chuzzle and his girls in any way.

_____ **Examining "White Privilege":** In a high school social studies class, a unit on diversity included lessons on "white privilege." A definition was given to students stating that in critical race theory, *white privilege* is a set of advantages that are believed to be enjoyed by white people beyond those commonly experienced by nonwhite people in the same social, political, and economic spaces (nation, community, workplace, income, etc.). In other words, it provides white people with "perks" that they do not earn and that people of color do not enjoy. For example, if I am a white person, when I am in a store, I don't have to worry about security personnel watching me closely or following me because of my skin color. In class, students were engaged in discussing their views about the existence of "white privilege" and its possible effects. Some parents in the community objected to the lessons, arguing that they were teaching white students that they should feel guilty and creating division and conflict among students. They questioned why the school would do something that could destroy the peace and goodwill between all races in the community. Should the school eliminate the lessons on "white privilege" and any discussion of the issue? Do lessons like this decrease or increase racial tensions and conflicts? Can a teacher decide independently to teach such lessons?

_____ **Make Someone Fall in Love:** A famous study by the provocative British psychologist Dr. Arthur Aron suggests that two people who have some basic traits in common can "fall in love" in a matter of minutes. In fact, it appears that following a few simple interactive behaviors a person can "make" someone else fall in love with him or her. The procedures involve sitting face to face with someone, asking a series of personal questions, and then staring into each other's eyes for four minutes. Of course, the participants have to be willing to follow these procedures. In a way, the protocol seems like the modern social psychology equivalent of a love potion. Intrigued by Dr. Aron's study, Diana Sabine hopes to follow the procedures with Fitzroy Hamilton ("Fitz" to his friends), whose locker is near Diana's. She hopes that she can at least influence him to ask her to prom. Diana's friend Beverly debunks Dr. Aron's claims and insists that the procedure will never work on Fitz. Diana's friend Roberta cautions Diana not to try, insisting that this form of manipulation robs a person of his will to choose a love interest freely. What should Diana do?

_____ **Marking Lynching Sites:** Bryan Stevenson, executive director of the Equal Justice Initiative, has initiated an effort to mark each of nearly four thousand sites of documented "racial terror lynchings" in the United States. Some of these sites are in the shadows of monuments to local community leaders who supported lynchings and may have initiated some of them. Mr. Stevenson hopes to place a memorial or marker at each site, noting that US residents should know that "lynching and the terror era shaped the geography, politics, economics and social characteristics of being black in America during the 20th century." In the town of Bedford, where it appears that ten particularly gruesome lynchings took place in the 1920s, many residents have resisted the idea of marking the spot to remember elements of a shameful history. The spot identified for the proposed marker is on the town square, which is public property. The Bedford Town Council would have to approve the installation of the marker. Should the Town Council acknowledge this dark period of the town's history or resist the installation in order to forget the crimes of the past and focus on a brighter, more harmonious future?

_____ **Building a Winning Character:** Coach Brian Katchum believes that playing sports as an adolescent is about dreams and democracy. As a baseball coach from Little League to high school, he believes the game is about hopes and character. His approach to coaching involves fluid batting orders, and infield as well as outfield innings for everyone on the team. If anyone on the team wants to pitch, he tells them that if they practice with their mom or dad, they will get to pitch an inning and maybe more. A poor fielder gets infield innings at second base. And a starting shortstop has some innings in right field. Pitchers get to pitch until they get three outs or four walks, whichever comes first. No one bats last for two games in a row. All players matter. There is no yelling, belittling, name-calling, manipulation, or criticism that could be characterized as mental abuse. Winning matters, but doing your best matters more. Memories matter the most. Coach Katchum reports that over his extensive career following this model he has had more wins than losses. Should all organized sports for youngsters up to age eighteen be required to follow the model of Coach Katchum, or will his methods end up hurting or holding back the development of talented players? Do his methods harm young athletes by shielding them from the realities of life—that everyone isn't always a winner and that talent is rewarded while poor performance is not?

Appendix B: Examining "White Privilege" in High School Classes

In eleventh-grade social studies classes at Robert A. Millikan High School, a unit on diversity includes lessons on "white privilege." Teachers and a supplementary text for the class define the concept by noting from critical race theory that *white privilege* is a set of advantages that are believed to be enjoyed by white people beyond those commonly experienced by nonwhite people in the same social, political, and economic spaces (nation, community, workplace, income, etc.). In other words, inherent privilege provides white people with "perks" that they do not earn and that people of color do not enjoy. For example, as support for the concept, theorists cite the example of shopping in a big retail store. Typically, a white shopper doesn't have to worry about security personnel watching closely or following the customer because of the color of the person's skin. In classes at Millikan High School, teachers assign students related readings and engage learners in discussing their views about the existence of "white privilege" and its possible effects.

Some skepticism: Some parents have objected to the lessons, arguing that they were teaching white students that they should feel guilty. The same parents claim that the discussions about white privilege create divisions and conflicts among students. The concerned parents question why the school would do something that could destroy the peace and goodwill among all races in the community. The objecting parents have organized and have demanded that the school board reevaluate the value and efficacy of the diversity curriculum that promulgates the concept of white privilege as an established fact.

Questions for Discussion: *Should the school board support the teaching of a diversity curriculum at Millikan High School that includes attention to the concept of white privilege?*

- For someone outside the community, how would you summarize what the controversy is about?

- What harm, if any, can come from teaching students about the concept of white privilege?
- Are the lessons that focus on the concept of white privilege likely to decrease or increase racial tensions and conflicts? What is the basis for your judgment?
- On what grounds can anyone justify the elimination of the lessons on white privilege and any discussion of the issue?
- How is it possible to continue to teach a diversity curriculum without attention to the concept of white privilege?
- To what extent can the concept of white privilege be taught as an established fact?
- What do the teachers who teach the diversity curriculum see as the advantages to teaching eleventh graders about the concept of white privilege?
- Can a teacher decide independently to teach such lessons?
- On balance, are there more benefits than disadvantages to teaching high school juniors about the concept of white privilege?

Academic Language

Language of the Case:

Racism
White privilege
Perk (perquisite)
Indoctrination
Discrimination
Color blindness

Language of the Directions:

Argument
Position
Point of view
Claim
Evidence
Reasoning (or Warrant)
Opposing argument

Related Readings:
"On Racism and White Privilege" from *Teaching Tolerance*
www.tolerance.org/article/racism-and-white-privilege

"'White Privilege' Lesson in Delavan-Darien High School Class in Wisconsin Draws Ire"
www.huffingtonpost.com/2013/01/16/white-privilege-class-at-_n_2489997.html

"Notre Dame's 'White Privilege Seminar': Racist Indoctrination or Education?"
www.csmonitor.com/USA/Society/2014/1208/Notre-Dame-s-White-Privilege-Seminar-Racist-indoctrination-or-education

---

Information Used as the Basis for the White Privilege Instruction at Millikan

On Racism

Racism is a doctrine or teaching, without scientific support, that does three things. First, it claims to find racial differences in things like character and intelligence. Second, racism asserts the superiority of one race over another or others. Finally, it seeks to maintain that dominance through a complex system of beliefs, behaviors, use of language, and policies. Racism ranges from the individual to the institutional level and reflects and enforces a pervasive view in white-dominated US culture that people of color are inferior to whites.

Racist beliefs include things like "white people are smarter than people of color," or "white people make better teachers." Racism can manifest itself in terms of individual behavior through hate crimes, or in institutional behavior through employment discrimination. Racism might manifest in individual language through the use of slurs, or in institutional policy through a school's selection of Eurocentric textbooks.

Related to these relatively obvious manifestations of racism is a subtle system that also contributes to the maintenance of the racial status quo. That subtle system is ***white skin privilege***.

On White Privilege

White skin privilege is not something that white people necessarily do, create, or enjoy on purpose. Unlike the more overt individual and institutional manifestations of racism described above, white skin privilege is a transparent preference for whiteness that saturates our society. White skin privilege serves several functions. First, it provides white people with "perks" that they do not earn and that people of color do not enjoy. Second, it creates real advantages for white people. White people either do not have to deal with a lot of challenges or possess more resources to address those challenges. Finally, white privilege shapes the world in which we all live—the way that we all navigate and interact with one another and with the world.

Video about White Privilege

https://www.facebook.com/UpworthyVideo/videos/785733804864502/
(This woman is at the grocery store with her half-white sister-in-law and the two women experience very different treatment by the same cashier within seconds of each other.)

White Privilege: The Perks

White people receive all kinds of perks as a function of their skin privilege. Consider the following:

- If I am a white person, when I cut my finger and go to the school or office's first aid kit, the "flesh-colored" Band-Aid generally matches my skin tone.
- If I am a white person, when I stay in a hotel, the complimentary shampoo generally works with the texture of my hair.
- If I am a white person, when I run to the store to buy pantyhose at the last minute, the "nude" color generally appears nude on my legs.
- If I am a white person, when I buy hair care products in a grocery store or drugstore, the shampoos and conditioners are in the aisle and section labeled "hair care" and not in a separate section for "ethnic products."
- If I am a white person, I can purchase travel-size bottles of hair care products at most grocery stores or drugstores.

White Privilege: The Advantages

Certainly, white privilege is not limited to perks like Band-Aids and hair care products. The second function of white skin privilege is that it creates significant advantages for white people. There are scores of things that a white person, generally, does not encounter, have to deal with, or even recognize. For example:

- If I am a white person, skin color does not work against me in terms of how people perceive my financial responsibility, style of dress, public speaking skills, or job performance.
- If I am a white person, people do not assume that I got where I am professionally because of my race (or because of affirmative action programs, which privilege the hiring of certain disadvantaged groups).
- If a nicely dressed white person is walking down the street late at night, people do not cross the street so as to avoid them for fear of being mugged or assaulted.
- If I am a white person, store security personnel or law enforcement officers do not harass me, pull me over, or follow me because of my race.
- If I am a white person eating at an expensive restaurant and I find out that the restaurant is cash only, the management will let me run to the ATM and get money.

White Privilege: The Worldview

The third thing that white privilege does is shape the way in which we view the world and the way in which the world views us. The perks and advantages described above are part of this phenomenon, but not all of it. Consider the following:

- If I am a white person, when I am told about our national heritage or "civilization," I am shown that people of my color made it what it is.
- If I am a white person, the schools that I attend or have attended use standard textbooks, which widely reflect people of my color and their contributions to the world.
- If I am a white person, when I look at the national currency or see photographs of monuments on the National Mall in Washington, DC, I see people of my race widely represented and celebrated.
- Courses about nonwhite cultures, history, or literature are generally "elective" rather than required courses.

Adapted from Teaching Tolerance
A Project of the Southern Poverty Law Center
www.tolerance.org/article/racism-and-white-privilege

Robert A. Millikan High School

Location: Hope, Illinois, a small city with a population of 150,000, eighty miles from a major metropolitan area

Mascot: Mustang

The football team has gone to their conference championships the last five years.

Girls' badminton has won two state championships.

The music department has won numerous awards for the last three years.

Faculty / Administration:

60 percent Female
40 percent Male

65 percent Caucasian
10 percent African American
10 percent Latinx
10 percent Asian
5 percent mixed

50 percent with bachelor's degrees
30 percent with master's degrees
20 percent beyond master's degrees

Five years and under teaching experience: 16 percent
Six to fourteen years teaching experience: 60 percent
Over fifteen years teaching experience: 24 percent

Student Information:

Reading and math: students scored slightly above state average
College bound: 70 percent
Graduation rate: 92 percent
Chronic truancy rate: slightly below state average
Average class size: 27
English language learners: 10 percent

60 percent Caucasian
20 percent Latinx
10 percent African American
5 percent Asian

1 percent Native American
4 percent mixed

50 percent eligible for free or reduced lunch

Information about the City:

One community college
One small private college
The city has had racial tensions in the past, but things have improved.
Recently, at the high school, a racial slur was scratched into a stall in the girls' student bathroom.

District Forum

Role-Playing

The Superintendent of the school district is holding a meeting to discuss whether Millikan High School should include instruction on the concept of white privilege in eleventh-grade social studies classes. The following people will give their arguments for or against the instruction, providing supporting evidence for their viewpoints.

Those in favor of the instruction about white privilege:

President of the Local Teachers' Union argues that everyone should support the school's social studies teachers who believe that understanding white privilege is crucial to the moral development of all students. The school district should respect the expertise of its social studies teachers, many of whom have master's degrees or beyond. They have been trained in social studies instruction and curriculum development and have consulted scholarly theory and research to apply in the classroom. The role of teachers is to prepare students for all obstacles they may face. Failing to teach about white privilege is not only detrimental to students of color but white peers as well.

Social Studies Department Chair is for the teaching of white privilege at the high school. S/he is aware of the impact skin color has played in the past and believes that students should be educated about recent incidents of racism. History books do not cover enough and are not necessarily up to date. Of the student population, some students are not pursuing a college education, so this is one of the last opportunities in school that these students have to learn about this pressing social topic.

Student Leader of Multicultural Club believes that students must learn to understand the people around them and themselves. Since white privilege is a social phenomenon, students cannot be expected to learn objectively through social or popular media. Students need to be made aware of white privilege in an educational setting. By choosing not to teach white privilege, society actually creates and perpetuates its existence.

Community College Professor/Parent is for the teaching of white privilege awareness lessons at the high school level because s/he sees issues relating to white privilege arise in higher education classrooms. Students at the community college also feel as if they would benefit from being exposed to and discussing these issues at an earlier age. In addition, the professor feels that exposing students to these ideas at an earlier age helps them to think critically, which is what higher education should be about. It also helps students learn how to interact with people of other cultures in real world environments. As a parent, s/he wants his or her children to be able to interact appropriately in a diverse society, and these lessons will contribute to that.

Those against the instruction about white privilege:

Parent is against the lessons about awareness of white privilege. S/he is concerned that high school curriculum should focus on teaching facts, reading, and writing rather than controversial issues. S/he argues that students should learn facts about historical events and the contributions people of color (such as Martin Luther King Jr., Cesar Chavez, Malala Yousafzai, and Malcolm X) have made to improving equality in the United States and worldwide. Schools should focus on teaching things everyone agrees on: reading, writing, facts, and positive historical contributions.

School Police Officer is concerned about maintaining harmony in the school and community. S/he argues against the instruction because it could easily create division by making white students feel shamed and suggesting they are guilty simply because they are white even if they haven't done anything to promote discrimination or inequality. The school should avoid anything that might lead to disharmony and conflict.

Social Studies Teacher is the only member of the department who is against the instruction. S/he argues that instead of teaching about white privilege schools should be teaching "color blindness"—that people should judge people by their character and not the color of their skin, ethnicity, religion, etc. Curriculum should explore and celebrate the similarities among all people rather than differences. People should be encouraged not to focus on a person's "color."

Dean of Students argues that controversial concepts such as "white privilege" are better dealt with in college rather than high school because a number of high school students may not be sophisticated enough to understand such a complex issue. Misconceptions by students can easily lead them to react in ways that actually increase conflicts among students and result in their feeling resentment toward others.

Follow-Up Writing

Write a letter to the Board of Education of Hope to convince them of your viewpoint on the issue of whether eleventh-grade social studies classes at Millikan High School should include instruction on the concept of white privilege. Provide specific supporting evidence for your viewpoint. Your letter will need to

- Introduce and explain the issue that you are writing about
- Provide specific evidence and reasoning to support your viewpoint
- Provide a response to arguments and evidence in opposition to (against) your viewpoint

Appendix C: Coding System

Pass 1 (surface or nonargumentative factors): sentence-based (number/percentage)
Pass 2 (argumentative factors): discourse-based (number)

PASS 1

Voice	**SV:**	Student voice
	TV:	Teacher voice
Conversational turn	**WT:**	words per conversational turn
	ST:	sentences per conversational turn
	WS:	words per sentence
Discussion	**P:**	noting procedures for the discussion
	SO:	socializing
Syntax	**SSS:**	using syntactic structures suggesting submissiveness or uncertainty
	SSA:	using syntactic structures suggesting confidence and/or assertiveness
Vocabulary	**V-R:**	using specific, varied vocabulary
	V-P:	using general, limited vocabulary
Manners	**I:**	interrupting a current speaker
	X:	treating other speakers with disrespect

1. **SV: Student voice (by conversational turn)**
2. **TV: Teacher voice (by conversational turn)**
3. **WT: words per conversational turn.**
4. **ST: sentences per conversational turn.**
5. **WS: words per sentence.**
6. **P: noting procedures for the discussion:**

   The speaker asks a procedural question or otherwise clarifies the task for the group. The speaker prompts others about some aspect of the task, including the reading from the material that has prompted the discussion.

e.g., (After a long discussion about whether robot can develop human intelligence.)

Student: I just have a question. Can we outsmart the robots? How much information do they know? Or do we know more information than them?

7. SO: socializing:

The speaker makes a strictly social comment that does not appear to contribute to the progress of the discussion.

e.g., What are you doing this weekend?

8. SSS: using syntactic structures suggesting tentativeness or uncertainty:

The speaker relies on tag question and pause, hemming, eh, etc. *Or the speaker asks a question as an expression of doubt.*

e.g., 1. Student 1: Do you think she would take a half of it?
Student 2: I would.

e.g., 2. Student 8: . . . It (robot) robs from our creativity. I don't know. Alex?

9. SSA: using syntactic structures suggesting a definitive stance:

The speaker relies on declarative statements, with little hesitation.

10. V-R: using specific, varied vocabulary:

The speaker uses varied and extensive vocabulary, multisyllable words, less common words, specific vs. general (e.g., vehicle, possessions vs. thing, stuff); uses metaphor or figurative words.

e.g., 1. Student 1: I don't think he actually knows what he is **committed** to.
Student 2: What is the **probability** of winning the lottery?

e.g., 2. Student: You said something about emotions. I feel like robots could actually replace emotions better than humans because they lack the **impatience**.

11. I: interrupting a current speaker:

The speaker does not want the current speaker to finish and interrupts the speaker currently speaking.

e.g., 1. Student 1: Since they are doing the reflection separately . . .
Student 2: Wait. Are they friends?

e.g., 2. Student 1: . . . It just kind of shows . . .
Ms. Torino: We can come back to you later.

12. X: treating other speakers with disrespect:

The speaker, through sarcasm, name-calling, ridicule, or dismissiveness, conveys disrespect for another speaker.

e.g., You idiot! How could you possibly think that? *(Not found)*

PASS 2

<table>
<tr><td rowspan="7">Claim making & supporting</td><td>C:</td><td>making a claim</td><td></td><td></td></tr>
<tr><td rowspan="4">D:</td><td rowspan="4">citing support for claim</td><td>DT:</td><td>support from texts</td></tr>
<tr><td>DP:</td><td>support from personal experience</td></tr>
<tr><td>DE:</td><td>support from invented example</td></tr>
<tr><td>DY:</td><td>testimony</td></tr>
<tr><td>W:</td><td>explaining/interpreting support for claim</td><td></td><td></td></tr>
<tr><td>B:</td><td>backing the interpretation</td><td></td><td></td></tr>
<tr><td rowspan="5">Over interactions: questioning, uptake, and summary (H, U, S)

Other: fragments and seeking clarification (F, L)</td><td>H:</td><td>challenging/questioning a claim</td><td></td><td></td></tr>
<tr><td>U:</td><td>practicing uptake</td><td></td><td></td></tr>
<tr><td>S:</td><td>summarizing a portion of the discussion</td><td></td><td></td></tr>
<tr><td>F:</td><td>uttering a fragmentary comment</td><td></td><td></td></tr>
<tr><td>L:</td><td>clarifying</td><td></td><td></td></tr>
</table>

1. C: making a claim:

The speaker asserts a claim (i.e., conclusion, generalization) relative to the focus for the discussion.

2. D: citing support for claim:

The speaker offers some form of data (e.g., actual or invented example, reference to a statement by an authority, statistical data, information) to support a claim.

3. W: explaining/interpreting support for claim:

The speaker explains the connection between expressed support and a claim. To connect claim and support, the speaker might cite a rule of thumb, a law of nature, a statute of government, an ethical principle, or a rule of an organization, like a school.

4. B: backing the interpretation:

The speaker cites support to suggest the legitimacy of a warrant for the interpretation of data.

e.g., Student 1: I was hoping that robots would get rid of a certain artistic aspect of learning; artistic as in the subject in general. (claim) In the *New York Times* article about Robo-Graders, it says, "or sentences that begin with 'or,' and sentences that start with 'and.' Nor sentence fragments. However, he said, e-Rater likes connectors like 'however' which serve as programming proxies for complex thinking." (cited evidence/data) This shows that it's programmed into the robots to take certain words over another word just because it's a difference word and not because it's more appropriate. (warrant/interpretation) It makes learning more formulaic than it is—you need to incorporate some degree of creativity and stylistic aspect into your writing than just formula enriched sentences that are better than others; absolutely better than others and not because it's not appropriate. (backing/support for warrant) DT: support from texts

e.g., Student 2: I agree with you. However, I feel the robot teachers will be good for social interaction because in "The Robot Teacher Connecting with Autistic Children" article. It says, "if the child selects incorrectly, the body language is subdued and he gives the child a consoling but encouraging message, urging them to try again." DT: support from texts

5. DP: support from personal experience

e.g., Student: I agree that for some classes having the robots could be kind of cool and could help kids to keep interest. Personally, I would only be interested the first day. It's like, "okay, cool. I get a robot teacher in class."

6. DE: support from invented example

e.g., Student: . . . If you take a general average of twenty students per classroom and 1 teacher per room, that's like ninety teachers who will be out of jobs if you employ the robots. How would you employ the teachers in the general area?

7. **DY: testimony, especially from simulated meeting in class**

e.g., I heard from someone that. . . .

8. **H: challenging/questioning a claim:**

The speaker challenges the claim, the accuracy or relevance of the support, or the legitimacy of a principle used to interpret support.

e.g., Student: Just kind of building off of that, I have to disagree.

9. **U: practicing uptake:**

The speaker recognizes the claim, argument or question expressed by another speaker in order to provide a context for a new contribution.

e.g., Student: So, you said something about robots teaching—not having ways to be able to teach students well.

10. **S: summarizing a portion of the discussion:**

The speaker summarizes what has been said as a means for affirming the status of the discussion. The summary involves more than the paraphrase of a single speaker.

e.g., Student: So, going back to the thing that Brianna and Jacqueline and Julie were talking just based off of how the robots are going to grade. *(class two)*

11. **F: uttering a fragmentary comment:**

The speaker offers a fragmentary statement, the purpose of which is unclear.

e.g., Student 1: But before that, he should go to the school and encourage them to cheer for their team.

Student 2: If they don't have people cheering for them. . . .

12. **L: clarifying:**

The speaker checks for understanding or affirms understanding, especially about what a conversational partner has said. This category includes a teacher's simple paraphrase of a speaker's contribution.

e.g., Student 23: So, going back to the thing that Brianna and Jacqueline and Julie were talking just based off of how the robots are going to grade. I think in that sense—I think what you guys are getting at is that it can be unfair if people are able to cheat the system. That's what you guys are worried about, right?

References

Applebee, A. N. (1996). *Curriculum as conversation: Transforming traditions of teaching and learning*. Chicago: The University of Chicago Press.

Applebee, A. N., & Langer, J. A. (2013). *Writing instruction that works: Proven methods for middle and high school classrooms*. New York: Teachers College Press.

Applebee, A. N., Langer, J. A., Nystrand, M., & Gamoran, A. (2003). Discussion-based approaches to developing understanding: Classroom instruction and student performance in middle and high school English. *American Educational Research Journal, 40*(3), 685–730.

Bakhtin, M. M. (1986). *Speech genres and other late essays*. M. Holquist & C. Emerson (Eds.). Austin: University of Texas Press.

Beers, G. K. (2003). *When kids can't read, what teachers can do: A guide for teachers, 6–12*. Portsmouth, NH: Heinemann.

Britton, J. (1983). Writing and the story of the world. In B. M. Kroll & C. G. Wells (Eds.), *Explorations in the development of writing: Theory, research, and practice* (pp. 3–30). New York: Wiley.

Burke, J. (2013). *The English teacher's companion: A completely new guide to classroom, curriculum, and the profession*. Portsmouth, NH: Heinemann.

Christensen, L. (2009). *Teaching for joy and justice: Re-imagining the language arts classroom*. Milwaukee, WI: Rethinking Schools.

Garcia, A., & O'Donnell-Allen, C. (2015). *Pose, wobble, flow: A culturally proactive approach to literacy instruction*. New York: Teachers College Press.

Hattie, J. (2009). *Visible learning: A synthesis of over 800 meta-analyses relating to achievement*. New York: Routledge.

Hillocks, G., Jr. (1995). *Teaching writing as reflective practice*. New York: Teachers College Press.

Hillocks, G., Jr. (1999). *Ways of thinking, ways of teaching*. New York: Teachers College Press.

Johannessen, L. R., Kahn, E. A., & Walter, C. C. (2009). *Writing about literature* (2nd ed.). Urbana, IL: National Council of Teachers of English.

Juzwik, M. M., Borsheim-Black, C., Caughlan, S., & Heintz, A. (2013). *Inspiring dialogue: Talking to learn in the English classroom*. New York: Teachers College Press.

Kahn, E. A. (1999). *What it takes to march to a different drummer: A study of six English teachers* (Unpublished doctoral dissertation). University of Chicago.

Kahn, E. A., McCann, T., Walter, C., Bouque, A., & Forde, D. (2017). *Can we talk about white privilege?* (Unpublished paper). NCTE Convention, St. Louis.

Kuhn, D. (1991). *The skills of argument*. New York: Cambridge University Press.

Langer, J. A. (2001). Beating the odds: Teaching middle and high school students to read and write well. *American Educational Research Journal*, *38*(4), 837–80.

McCann, T. M. (2014). *Transforming talk into text: Argument writing, inquiry, and discussion, grades 6–12*. New York: Teachers College Press.

McCann, T. M., D'Angelo, R., Galas, M., & Greska, M. (2015). *Literacy and history in action: Immersive approaches to disciplinary thinking, grades 5–12*. New York: Teachers College Press.

McCann, T. M., Johannessen, L. R., Kahn, E., & Flanagan, J. M. (2006). *Talking in class: Using discussion to enhance teaching and learning*. Urbana, IL: National Council of Teachers of English.

McIntosh, P. (1989, July/August). White privilege: Unpacking the invisible knapsack. *Peace and Freedom Magazine*. Retrieved from https://nationalseedproject.org/white-privilege-unpacking-the-invisible-knapsack.

Mercier, H., & Sperber, D. (2011). Why do humans reason? Arguments for an argumentative theory. *Behavioral and Brain Sciences*, *34*, 57–111.

Mercier, H., & Sperber, D. (2017). *The enigma of reason*. Cambridge, MA: Harvard University Press.

Morrison, T. (2007). *The bluest eye*. New York, NY: Vintage International.

Newell, G. E., Bloome, D., & Hirvela, A. (2015). *Teaching and learning argumentative writing in high school English language arts classrooms*. New York: Routledge.

Nystrand, M. (1997). *Opening dialogue: Understanding the dynamics of language and learning in the English classroom*. New York: Teachers College Press.

Nystrand, M. (2006). Research on the role of classroom discourse as it affects reading comprehension. *Research in the Teaching of English*, *40* (4), 392–412.

Nystrand, M. (2017). *Twenty acres: Events that transform us*. Madison, WI: Wisconsin Center for Education Research. Retrieved from http://class.wceruw.org/documents/Twenty%20Acres.pdf.

O'Donnell-Allen, C. (2011). *Tough talk, tough texts: Teaching English to change the world*. Portsmouth, NH: Heinemann.

Rankine, C. (2014). *Citizen: An American lyric*. Minneapolis, MN: Graywolf Press.

Singleton, G. (1992). *Courageous conversations about race*. Retrieved from http://courageousconversation.com.

Smagorinsky, P. (2018). Emotion, reason, and argument: Teaching persuasive writing in tense times. *English Journal, 107*(5), 98–101.

Smith, M. W., & Wilhelm, J. D. (2010). *Fresh takes on teaching literary elements: How to teach what really matters about character, setting, point of view, and theme*. New York: Scholastic.

Stern, D. (1995). *Teaching English so it matters: Creating curriculum for and with high school students*. Thousand Oaks, CA: Corwin Press.

Troyka, L. Q. (1974). *A study of the effect of simulation-gaming on expository prose competence of college remedial English composition students* (Doctoral dissertation). New York University. Retrieved from ERIC Document Reproduction Service. (No. ED090541)

Troyka, L. Q., & Nudelman, J. (1975). *Taking action: Writing, reading, speaking, and listening through simulation-games*. Englewood Cliffs, NJ: Prentice-Hall.

Turkle, S. (2015). *Reclaiming conversation*. New York: Penguin Books.

Tyler, R. W. (1969). *Basic principles of curriculum and instruction*. Chicago: University of Chicago Press.

University of Michigan School of Education. (n.d.). High leverage practices. *Teaching Works*. Retrieved from http://www.teachingworks.org/work-of-teaching/high-leverage-practices.

VanDerHeide, J., & Newell, G. E. (2013). Instructional chains as a method for examining the teaching and learning of argumentative writing in classrooms. *Written Communication, 30*(3), 300–329.

Vygotsky, L. (1996). *Thought and language*. A. Kozulin (Ed.). Cambridge, MA: MIT Press.

Walsh, R. (2017, September 13). Questions as invitations, not inquisitions. *Russ on Reading* (blog). Retrieved from http://russonreading.blogspot.com/2017/09/questions-as-invitations-not.html.

Wiggins, G. P., & McTighe, J. (2005). *Understanding by design*. Alexandria, VA: Association for Supervision and Curriculum Development.

Wilhelm, J. D. (2016). *"You gotta BE the book": Teaching engaged and reflective reading with adolescents* (3rd ed.). New York: Teachers College Press.

Wilhelm, J. D., Douglas, W., & Fry, S. W. (2014). *The activist learner: Inquiry, literacy, and service to make learning matter*. New York: Teachers College Press.

Wilhelm, J. D., Fransen, S., & Smith, M. W. (2014). *Reading unbound: Why kids need to read what they want—and why we should let them*. New York: Scholastic.

Wilhelm, J. D., & Novak, B. (2011). *Teaching literacy for love and wisdom: Being the book and being the change*. New York: Teachers College Press.

Yang, G. L. (2006). *American born Chinese*. New York: First Second Books.

Index

Authors

Elizabeth A. Kahn taught English language arts for thirty-six years and served as English department chair. She is currently teaching in the English teacher education program at Northern Illinois University in DeKalb, Illinois. She is coauthor of *The Dynamics of Writing Instruction* (2010) and *The Dynamics of Writing Instruction Series* (2011–12), *Writing about Literature* (1984 and 2009, updated edition), *Talking in Class: Using Discussion to Enhance Teaching and Learning* (2006), and *Designing and Sequencing Prewriting Activities* (1982), and coeditor of *Reflective Teaching, Reflective Learning* (2005). She has authored or coauthored numerous journal articles and is a frequent presenter at NCTE and IATE conferences. She has served as president of the Illinois Association of Teachers of English (IATE) and on the NCTE Secondary Section Steering Committee and the Executive Committee of the Conference on English Education. She received a PhD in education from The University of Chicago and was a National Board Certified Teacher.

Thomas M. McCann is a professor of English at Northern Illinois University, where he contributes to the teacher licensure program. He taught English in high schools for twenty-five years, including seven years working in an alternative high school. His books include *Transforming Talk into Text* (2014) and *Literacy and History in Action* (2015). His coauthored books include *Talking in Class* (2006), *The Dynamics of Writing Instruction* (2010), and *Teaching Matters Most* (2012).

Carolyn C. Walter supervises student teachers for Northern Illinois University. Previously, she taught English students for thirty years at both public and private high schools. During that time, she taught students of all ages and ability levels, but she reserves a special place in her heart for ninth graders. Walter has enjoyed professional involvement by presenting at local, state, and national conferences and workshops over more than three decades and has coauthored *Writing and Designing Pre-Writing Activities* and *Writing about Literature*, first and second editions, as well as several articles. She earned her BA from The College of Wooster and her MAT from The University of Chicago.

This book was typeset in TheMix and Palatino by Barbara Frazier.

Typefaces used on the cover include Raleway and Avenir.

The book was printed on 50-lb. White Offset paper by King Printing Company, Inc.